A THEATRICAL FEAST

by

Elizabeth Sharland

Touching on the lives and works of London's Legendary Actors, Writers and Playwrights

A Compendium of Fact, Fiction and Favourite places of the Theatrical and Literary personalities of the Golden Era in the West End

Reports from Laurence Olivier, Vivien Leigh, Noel Coward, Ralph Richardson, Alec Guinness, Graham Greene and other theatre celebrities on their favourite food and places in London as well as contributing signed recipes.

BARBICAN PRESS

British Library Cataloguing in Publication Data
A catalogue record for this book is available from the British Library

ISBN 0-9531930-2-0

Typeset by Amolibros, Watchet, Somerset
This book production has been managed by Amolibros
Printed and bound by Professional Book Supplies, Oxford, England

Table of Contents

List of Illustrations   iv
Introduction   v
Acknowledgements   vi
Foreword   vii
Prologue   ix
Chapter One   Covent Garden   1
Chapter Two   Suppers at the Lyceum Theatre – Henry Irving   5
Chapter Three   George Arliss   10
Chapter Four   James Agate   14
Chapter Five   Historic London Theatrical Restaurants   16
Chapter Six   George Bernard Shaw and *The Applecart*   29
Chapter Seven   John Gielgud   33
Chapter Eight   John Betjeman   36
Chapter Nine   John Galsworthy   39
Chapter Ten   Rupert Brooke   41
Chapter Eleven   Somerset Maugham – *Cakes and Ale*   43
Chapter Twelve   Terence Rattigan   45
Chapter Thirteen   Gala: Sybil Thorndike and Lewis Casson   47
Chapter Fourteen   Alec Guinness   51
Chapter Fifteen   Sydney Smith, 1771-1845   54
Chapter Sixteen   Vivien Leigh   56
Chapter Seventeen   Afternoon Tea and Chocolates   58
Chapter Eighteen   Sausages on Stage   60
Chapter Nineteen   P G Wodehouse   62
Chapter Twenty   Following in Noel Coward's Footsteps   65
Chapter Twenty-one   Robert Morley   67
Chapter Twenty-two   Judy Campbell   72
Chapter Twenty-three Judi Dench   74
Chapter Twenty-four Celebrity Recipes   77
Chapter Twenty-five A Short History of London Theatre 1900 to 1970   86
Epilogue   111
Personal Comments   116

List of Illustrations

Illustrations 1-18 facing page 46, illustrations 19-28 facing page 78.

1 Lilian Baylis, c 1933, with other guests including Charles Laughton, and James Mason.
2 1st May 1956, celebration at Binkie Beaumont's home at 14 Lord North Street in honour of Dame Sybil joining the Phoenix Theatre Company, with Paul Scofield, Sybil Thorndike, Lewis Casson and Peter Brook.
3 At the Ivy: Vivien Leigh, Kay Kendall, Lauren Bacall with Noel Coward.
4 John Miller with Sir John Gielgud.
5 Author with Kenneth Branagh at Criterion Gala for Sir John Gielgud after the showing of his film, *Swan Song.*
6 Simpsons-in-the-Strand, interior.
7 Criterion Restaurant.
8 The Salisbury, St Martin's Lane.
9 Simpsons-in-the-Strand, entrance.
10 The Ivy.
11 Sheekey's in St Martin's Court.
12 Julian Slade with Michael Law.
13 The author with Lord Richard Attenborough at the Ivy.
14 The Grill Room at the Café Royal.
15 Alexander H Cohen with Sir John Gielgud and Vivien Leigh.
16 Kaspar the cat at the Savoy.
17 An original cocktail shaker which was used in the American bar in the 1930s.
18 Vivien Leigh, a painting by Gary George.
19 Rules: public door on left, door for Royalty on right.
20 Margaret Thatcher at Rules.
21 The Greene Room.
22 Charles Dickens Room at Rules.
23 The entrance to the Charles Dickens Room.
24 Rules: caricature of Sir Noel Coward.
25 The alcove where Edward VII entertained the actress Lily Langtree.
26 Interior of John Betjeman Room.
27 Sir John Gielgud's favourite table at Rules.
28 Launch of the first book in this series at Rules.

Introduction

"There are only 365 dinners a year, and I don't see why I should eat a bad one," declared Duff Cooper, who had the luck to enjoy a spell as Ambassador in Paris, the gastronomic capital of the world. Elizabeth Sharland's latest book would have held considerable appeal to Duff Cooper, who would certainly have agreed that a night at the theatre needs to be rounded off with a delicious dinner.

This book evokes a lost era. Those were the days when the star not only dazzled on stage, but made a second entrance, in full evening dress, at the restaurant. The friends would be waiting and the party would go on late into the night. How different from today! Now the departing stars leave the stage door in blue jeans and head off in dreary little cars, or on motorbikes or bicycles, or even foot it to the Underground.

Elizabeth allows us to escape back to the days of elegance, legendary theatrical couples like the Oliviers, Vivien Leigh holding court at the table, still boasting a tiny waist, despite the delicious food on offer, Noel Coward, cigarette holder to the fore, John Gielgud famously and unintentionally letting unwelcome home truths slip out in total innocence.

The joy of it all is that it is still possible to dine at the Ivy, or the Caprice, the Savoy Grill or famous old Rules and you will find the atmosphere unchanged. Soho still has the Gay Hussar in Frith Street and Quo Vadis, where many movie deals have come to life.

"A good cook is like a sorcerer who dispenses happiness," wrote Elsa Schiaparelli, the legendary dress designer. So too a good author, I suggest. Elizabeth Sharland is that and more. She is also a musician, an artist, a pianist, a traveller, and a playwright. Who better to guide us to a feast in London's Theatreland?

Hugo Vickers
August 2001

Acknowledgements

The author acknowledges the help of Richard Mangan at Mander & Mitchenson for finding some of the photographs. Also many thanks to the estates of the following people for permission to quote from books and articles:

Sheridan Morley for permission to use material from *Morley Marvels* by Robert Morley edited by Sheridan Morley. *Up the Years from Bloomsbury* by George Arliss (1926), *The Unholy Trade* by Richard Findlater, Terence Rattigan, P G Wodehouse, John Casson, Alec Guinness and Laurence Irving, Rupert Brooke. Grateful thanks to Hugo Vickers, John Miller, Gary O'Connor, Barry Day, Paul Webb, Ricky McMenemy at Rules, Nicola Gold at the Savoy Hotel, to my editor Jane Tatam, and to my husband Gerald who did all the computer work.

Every effort has been made to trace all copyright holders, but if any have inadvertently been overlooked, the author and publishers will be pleased to make the necessary arrangements at the first opportunity.

Dedicated to

Franco Zeffirelli

Foreword

It does not surprise me that, in this her latest venture, Elizabeth Sharland has decided to study the history of actors and their abiding interest in the culinary arts. Somehow, it seems quite natural to me that anyone interested in the theatre should also be moved emotionally by the kitchen arts. Maybe most of us are more identified with Falstaff and his famous appetite than with actually mastering any aspect of cooking.

The reader of this book will, I am sure, ask for a second helping of stories of equally famous actors and their culinary appetites. In *A Theatrical Feast*, she weaves recipes, accounts of famous restaurants and their theatrical clientele, poetry, quotations and anecdotes by such legends as Oscar Wilde, George Bernard Shaw, Vivien Leigh and Sir John Gielgud. This is literally a feast that skilfully brings together the fascinating worlds of acting and the culinary arts.

John Gander

(John Gander is the former restaurant critic for The Kensington & Chelsea Post, The Palm Beach Post *and* The Palm Beach Illustrated.*)*

"Elizabeth Sharland's Feast of Delights leaves me hungry for more of my favourite people in my favourite places." Barrie Ingham

Prologue to George Farquahar's
The Inconstant, or The Way to Win Him, at Drury Lane

Like hungry guests a sitting audience looks,
Plays are like suppers: poets are the cooks.
The founders you; the table is this place.
The carvers we, the prologue is the grace.
Each act, a course; each scene, a different dish.
Though we're in Lent, I doubt you're still
    for flesh—
Satire's the sauce, high-seasoned, sharp, and
    rough:
Kind masques and beaux, I hope you're
    pepper-proof.
Wit is the wine; but 'tis so scarce the true,
Poets, like vintners, balderdash and brew.

Your surly scenes, where rant and bloodshed
    join,
Are butcher's meat, a battle's a sirloin.
Your scenes of love, so flowing, soft, and
    chaste,
Are water-gruel, without salt or taste.
Bawdy's fat venison, which, too stale, can
    please;
Your rakes love hogoes like your damned
    French cheese.
Your rarity for the fair guests to gape on
Is your nice squeaker, or Italian capon;
Or your French virgin-pullet, garnished
    round
And dressed with sauce of some—four
hundred pound.

An opera, like an olio, nicks the age;
Farce is the hasty-pudding of the stage.
For when you're treated with indifferent
    cheer,
Ye can dispense with slender stage-coach
    fare.
A pastoral's whipped cream; stage-whims,
    mere trash;
And tragi-comedy, half fish, half flesh.
But comedy, that, that's the darling cheer.
This night we hope you'll an Inconstant bear;
Wild fowl is liked in playhouse all the year.

Yet since each mind betrays a different taste,
And every dish scarce pleases every guest,
If ought you relish, do not damn the rest.
This favour craved, up let the music strike:
You're welcome all—now fall to where you
    like!

Peter Motteux (1702)

Prologue

The first scene in the musical *My Fair Lady* takes place in Covent Garden. Rex Harrison hears Julie Andrews speaking in a cockney accent or rather Henry Higgins hears Eliza Doolittle – and the rest is history. Both Rex Harrison and Julie Andrews would remember the area when it was a vegetable market with fruit, flowers and produce being sold from the very early hours of the morning, the whole area full of colourful characters and masses of flowers and vegetables. They would know the little cafes and restaurants down all the narrow side-streets, many of which are still there even though the market has gone. So would George Bernard Shaw years before, when he lived in Adelphi Terrace.

In one of these streets, Maiden Lane, is the oldest restaurant in London, Rules, which is full of theatrical treasures, where Charles Dickens used to dine, and more recently Graham Greene and Noel Coward. It has a history of scandal, celebrities and good food. St Paul's, the Actors' Church, is nearby, with its own garden and the church full of memorial plaques for famous actors most of whom knew and loved the restaurants in this area.

As London changes and the generation of actors who knew Covent Garden when it was a market and who dined in the area is gradually disappearing, as well as the playwrights who knew the Ivy and Sheekey's before these restaurants became celebrated, extracts from their writings, diaries and articles about the various places they frequented when not working remind us of that era. This book includes a collection of their work to rediscover the charm and brilliance of their poems, anecdotes and prose, particularly about their favourite food and eating places.

From Henry Irving's historic suppers held on stage at the Lyceum Theatre to Graham Greene celebrating his birthdays at Rules and mentioning the restaurant in *The End of the Affair*, both actors and writers acknowledge that eating and drinking were a large part of their lives.

The late Warner Le Roy, whose restaurants of New York included Tavern on the Green and the Russian Tea Room said, "A restaurant is a fantasy, a kind of living theater in which diners are the most important members of the cast. It is one of the few creations that appeal to all of the senses and one with which I can create my own world."

Thespians who like to follow in their footsteps and read a collection of the celebrities' reports in this book may create their own memories of all the places where excellent browsing and sluicing went on. But don't forget the more humble spots where struggling thespians licked their wounds, if not much else, and kept body and soul together while "resting". Noel Coward wrote that he remembered the Ivy when it had linoleum on the floor and the manager often gave him credit when he needed it.

Theatre lovers who like to follow in their footsteps can read this collection of extracts and descriptions as a suggestion as to where to create their own memories.

At the back of the book there is space to write in your own special places and meals you may want to remember, as well as the play you attended or the book you were reading that day.

CHAPTER ONE

Covent Garden

The spiritual energy of creative people over centuries lingers on over Covent Garden. Even now, you sense it though the piazza is full of tourists and street performers, and loud music, sometimes a carousel playing. Perhaps the best time to feel these spirits in such old streets and buildings is early in the morning or late at night when the crowds have dispersed. All the great actors trod these streets, and you can imagine the aspirations and ambitions that these artists had, either on their way to and from the theatre or celebrating at a restaurant during the run of a play.

This part of London is unique, no other district is quite the same. The tiny alleys and courtyards are sometimes missed unless you take the time to find them, and they are tucked away, through archways and doorways that are difficult to find. Godwin Court is one of them, a tiny row of bow-windowed houses off St Martin's Lane, where the famed literary agent, Margaret Ramsay, had her office. Present-day playwrights such as David Hare and Simon Callow write about their visits to her office, when she seemed to be the only agent who was promoting new plays. This row of houses seem to be straight out of a Charles Dickens novel, and, on a misty early-morning walking there, you could easily feel you were living a hundred years ago.

Alan Dent, a theatre critic, wrote in his book about Covent Garden of a ghost he saw walking down the Strand. His description is eerily full of reality. He walked behind this old lady, who was in a period costume, and then quickly passed her, so he could look back and see her face. When he turned to view her, she had gone.

The Actors' Church is right in the middle of the most sacred area of Covent Garden. It is here that many of the memorial services are held for famous actors.

If ever a theatrical inspiration from the past is needed, a walk through the church will inspire any drama student. The plaques on the wall, the benches in the garden with their plaques of dedication are there to be seen by all. There is something about the combination of the climate—the fresh early morning—and the old cobblestones, the atmosphere of the old garden, which is a joy, that must have stimulated Irving, Garrick, Kean and the core of the acting profession.

Every drama schoolteacher should arrange for students to be taken there as part of their training in the tradition and history of English theatre. You can read the biographers who tell of their activities in this area. George Bernard Shaw lived in Adelphi Terrace, now unfortunately no longer there, just on the other side of The Strand, but he spent his days in and around this area. He was married in Henrietta Street, which is one of the most famous streets in Covent Garden. Fanny Kelly lived there as did the actress who, when not working, made gowns for the Royal Family, as she was also a brilliant dressmaker. There is a long list of famous writers and performers who lived on this street, not all documented as yet, but details are to be found in their letters and diaries.

Charles Lamb, the English essayist and critic, fell in love with the actress, Fanny Kelly. Fanny owes her immortality to him through his writings. He said he adored her and here is his letter of proposal to her in 1819...

Dear Miss Kelly,

We had the pleasure... "pain" I might better call it, of seeing you last night in the new play.

It was a most consummate piece of acting, but what a task for you to undergo. It has given rise to a train of thinking which I cannot suppress.

Would to God you were released from this way of life, that you could bring your mind to consent to take your lot with us and throw off for ever the whole burden of your existence, and come and be a reality to us! Can you leave off harassing yourself to please a thankless multitude who know nothing of you and begin at last to live to yourself and your friends?

I have quite income enough, if that were all, to justify for me making such a proposal with what I may call even a handsome provision for my survivor.

As plainly and frankly as I have seen you give or refuse assent in some feigned scene, so frankly do me the justice to answer me.

This was her reply: she wrote this letter to Charles Lamb from 4 Henrietta Street after his proposal of marriage...

"Henrietta Street, 20th July 1819

An early and deeply rooted attachment to the theatre has fixed my heart on one from whom no worldly prospect can well induce me to withdraw it. But, while I thus frankly and decidedly decline your proposal, believe me, I am not insensible to the high honour which the preference of such a mind as yours confers on me.

Living in this area I became interested in every aspect of these historical theatrical figures, and after studying their work, the plays, their productions and performances, I also developed an interest in where they relaxed and where they met after work, whether coffee-houses, restaurants or bars. This led me to hunt out their haunts, mostly in the same area.

The Restoration marked the first appearance of women upon the stage. Until then, boy actors played the women's parts, since even then actors were somewhat disreputable, and the stage was not considered a suitable occupation for a respectable woman. The boys learned their craft in this way, which was the apprenticeship they had. Nell Gwynn was born in 1650 and died at the age of thirty-seven. She was one actress who did give up the theatre for another life. She was probably the best known actress in the Restoration theatre, but she gave it all up at the age of twenty to live a more luxurious life. She had been very poor and started her career by selling oranges in Drury Lane. She became more famous as a courtesan and, as we all know, was the mistress of Charles II, to name but one. John Dryden wrote this epilogue to his tyrannic love called "Nelly's Ghost".

I come, kind gentlemen, strange news to tell ye;
I am the ghost of poor departed Nelly.
Sweet ladies, be not frighted, I'll be civil;
I'm what I was, a little harmless devil.
For, after death, we sprites have just such natures
We had, for all the world, when human creatures;
And, therefore, I, that was an actress here,
Play all my tricks in hell, a goblin there
Gallants, look to't, you say there are no sprites;
But I'll come dance about your beds at nights.
And faith you'll be in a sweet kind of taking
When I surprise you between sleep and waking.
To tell you true, I walk, because I die
Out of my calling, in a tragedy.
O Poet, damned dull poet, who could prove
So senseless, to make Nelly die for love!
Nay, what's yet worse, to kill me in the prime
Of Easter-term, in tart and cheese-cake time!
I'll fit the fop; for I'll not one word say,
To excuse his godly, out-of-fashion play;
A play, which, if you dare but twice sit it out,
You'll be slandered, and be thought devout.
But, farewell, gentlemen, and make haste to me,

I'm sure ere long to have your company.
And for my epitaph when I am gone,
I'll trust no poet, but will write my own…
Here Nelly lies, who, though she lived a slattern,
She died a princess, acting in Saint Catherine.

In this book, there are descriptions of the places actors frequented. Even though many of the theatres are now gone, many of the restaurants, such as Rules, still remain. The Coal Hole on the Strand is still frequented by great actors. Richard Harris used to drink with Richard Burton after Burton had played Hamlet at the Old Vic across Waterloo Bridge. It was supposed to have been a brothel at one time, but obviously became respectable a century later.

The Strand Palace Hotel in The Strand originally had a white marble foyer and staircase with art deco passageways to the gift shops on the ground floor. It is now totally renovated, and the distinctive features have all but disappeared. Many distinguished actors stayed there, as well as at the Savoy, but the latter has fortunately kept most of its historical features.

Actors' work is ephemeral. Composers, painters, writers, sculptors—all leave their work behind, so that you can admire and analyse it, but even though the great interpreters of music, pianists, instrumentalists and conductors, are lost, there is always the haunting curiosity as to whether their interpretations would hold up today. But at least we have the architecture as well as some of the theatres. It would be interesting to know when the existing theatres, which now house all the ghosts of these great actors, are demolished in the twenty-first century—the Phoenix, the Haymarket, the Shaftesbury among them—what kind of theatres will be built in their place, if any at all.

Frank Matcham built the magnificent Coliseum and Palladium, and they can't last forever, so we hope that some part of them may be left, such as the front portico of the Haymarket, for example, rather than it being replaced with totally new, modern steel and glass performance spaces.

Oscar Wilde said…
I always pass on good advice. It is the only thing to do with it. It is never of any use to oneself.

Thirty-five is a very attractive age. London society is full of women of the very highest birth who have, of their own free choice, remained thirty-five for years.

CHAPTER TWO

Suppers at the Lyceum Theatre

Today, the Lyceum Theatre in Covent Garden has been restored to its former glory. Cameron Mackintosh rescued it from years of neglect, since it had been boarded up for many years. It now is the home of the mega-hits of Andrew Lloyd Webber, and these two men must be congratulated for restoring one of London's most famous theatres. A hundred years ago, Britain's foremost actor, Henry Irving, leased the theatre, and as a famous actor/manager, made history with his partnership with the actress Ellen Terry.

Born in Somerset in 1836, he was brought up by a Methodist aunt in Cornwall, and he was intended for a respectable clerical career, but was stubbornly stage-struck. He changed his name to Irving from Broadribb. He was the first actor to be knighted. It was his reward for his years of management of the Lyceum Theatre which began in 1878 and lasted to his death.

However, his personal life, as for so many, was not happy. On the night of his greatest triumph, as Mathias in *The Bells* (a play by the French writer Chatrain), he was riding home in his carriage with his wife, and as they passed Hyde Park Corner she said to him, "I hope you're not going to go on making a fool of yourself for the rest of your life." It was the night he left her and their marriage. He never spoke to her again, but always left seats for her in a box on every opening night. He was a magnificent showman; his best Shakespearean roles were Shylock, Iago and Benedick.

After many tours around England and the States, Irving felt he was now, in 1878, celebrated enough to take over the management of the Lyceum.

In September 1879 Irving returned from Venice where he had been working on the character of Shylock, having left instructions for the backstage lumber-rooms at the Lyceum to be cleared out. Irving intended to have them restored to their former glory as the meeting-place of a dining society, the Sublime Society of Beefsteaks, whose membership had included the dramatist Sheridan, the composer Samuel Arnold and the composer of melodramatic oratorios, Perry, as well as members of the aristocracy such as Lord Erskine and the Duke of Norfolk who had been the first President of the Society. The staple diet, as the society's name indicated, was beefsteak which was carved by the president; the drinks were beer and port.

Apart from a new kitchen, additions included the earliest portraits and busts acquired by Irving, which formed the nucleus of his great collection. At the first supper given by Irving shortly after the beginning of the 1879-80 season, champagne and brandy were served instead of the earlier beer and port. At this event, Irving announced his intention of playing Shylock that season.

In February 1880, to commemorate the one hundredth performance of *The Merchant of Venice*, Irving invited some three hundred guests to a dinner in the Beefsteak Rooms of the Lyceum. Oscar Wilde was among them, as well as other dramatists, musicians, critics and painters, artists of all kinds mingled with people from the highest ranks of society, all of whom were received by Irving and Ellen Terry. The dinner consisted of five courses washed down with plenty of Heidsieck champagne. Irving sat at the head of the table. At his side were Lord Londesborough, who had recently lost a hundred thousand pounds backing Boucicault's musical comedy *Babil and Bijou*, and Lord Houghton, who was to propose the customary toast to Irving's health. However the latter, to general surprise and irritation, indulged his not very great wit at the expense of his host and some of the other guests, by criticising the fondness on the part of managers and actors (presumably including Irving) for long runs, and also criticising Irving's sympathetic portrayal of Shylock. Irving replied with a witty speech, vigorously defending himself, and proposed a new play, to be entitled *The After-life of Shylock,* which would feature an even more sympathetic Shylock. His audience cheered him loudly. The evening went on till dawn. *The Merchant of Venice* ran for seven months.

Two years later, again on the one hundredth night, this time of *Romeo and Juliet*, Irving threw another party, a banquet in fact, on the stage of the Lyceum, which had been transformed into a garden by moonlight, the auditorium being hidden behind a veil of green gauze. The company included an American impresario, Henry E Abbey, and Lord Houghton was replaced by the Earl of Lytton, who, in his toast to Irving's health, did not repeat the gaucherie of his predecessor.

The question of the long runs of plays was again raised in Irving's speech of thanks, and he admitted the tedium it engendered in the actor and the difficulty of maintaining the same high standards of performance that were possible in short runs or in a repertory schedule. He also announced his forthcoming tour of America, which started in October of the following year, 1883.

In 1902 he made a second American tour that was even more successful than the first. On his return, however, he received some bad news. The London County Council had embarked on strict enforcement of the regulations about fire prevention in theatres, with the result that the Lyceum would be forced to close unless very expensive renovations were undertaken, which the shareholders found themselves unable to afford. Irving himself tried to raise the necessary capital without success, so he knew his beloved theatre was doomed.

Meanwhile London was preparing for the coronation of King Edward VII. Irving, in the past, had done much to recall to the theatre the intellectual and middle-class public and to overcome their old prejudices against his profession. It is doubtful if he could have done so had he not, at the very outset of his campaign, had the private encouragement and public approval of Albert Edward, Prince of Wales. Through the courteous entertainment of actors at his own table and through the gracious acceptance of their hospitality in return, the prince had endorsed Irving's claims for his profession and had indicated to a society prone to trim its opinions to those of the Court that actors were no longer to be considered as being beyond the pale of respectability. His patronage was the expression of a genuine love of the theatre. He was equally at home and at his ease in Toole's dressing-room or behind the scenes of the Lyceum, discussing technicalities with the master machinist. Above all, he appreciated and admired Irving's simple loyalty and integrity, rightly assessing his value to the kingdom over which he would ultimately reign. Irving knew how much he owed to the friendly gestures and sage advice that had been extended to him from Marlborough House. Now, if ever, was the moment to give public expression to his gratitude. That the enthronement of his patron and his own dethronement happened to coincide was not to be deplored but rather to be welcomed as an excuse for according the Lyceum obsequies of unparalleled splendour.

Already rajahs, sultans, tribal chiefs and potentates of every shade and degree were converging on London from the furthest corners of the empire. Irving, as usual, considered them in terms of the Lyceum. Here was material for a noble and glittering assembly such as had never been seen on the Lyceum or on any other stage. Heedless of his empty purse, disregarding the need to make provision for his old age, he wrote to the Lord Chamberlain to ask if a gala performance, followed by a reception on the stage of the visiting princes and their suites, would be acceptable to His Majesty. The king not only welcomed the idea but instantly directed the Indian and Colonial Offices to see that these plans were effectively set in motion. The date decreed by the authorities for the entertainment was 3rd July. Thus, as far as the public was concerned, Irving would surrender his sovereignty of the Lyceum on 19th July, not in the sombre twilight of chagrin and bankruptcy, but in a radiance which would typify and even surpass the past splendours of his long and illustrious reign.

On 26th June, owing to the king's sudden illness, the coronation was postponed. Those, however, who were responsible for the entertainment of so many distinguished visitors were instructed officially to fulfil the engagements they had made. So on the night of 3rd July, Irving played *Waterloo* and *The Bells* to a resplendent and heterogeneous audience, which at the end of the performance surged into the corridors and foyers of the Lyceum where they waited until Stoker's magical transformation of the stage and the auditorium was completed.

At his command, regiments of carpenters gutted the stalls and pit, hurling the seats into carts waiting at the exits; a tornado of cleaners swept up behind them and on their heels upholsterers laid a field of crimson carpet. While workers bridged the orchestra with an imposing staircase, the florists planted a jungle of palms, exotic flowers and shrubs that would make the most equatorial chieftain feel at home. In a trice, the stage was cleared of scenery and properties, and the vast naked walls hung with scarlet draperies. Great chandeliers were hoisted aloft, and over the proscenium glowed a monstrous Union Jack surmounted by a crown in coloured electric lights (electricity was convenient for nonsense of this kind). Meanwhile, perhaps to Stoker's special delight, a posse of detectives rummaged every corner of the theatre for anarchists and, having drawn a disappointing blank, posted themselves at the entrances to see that among the guests there were no thieves tempted to pluck a ruby from a passing turban or diamonds from the jewel-studded rajahs, some of whom were said to be worth half a million as they stood. This transformation seemed to have been instantaneous. In fact, only forty minutes had elapsed when Irving took his stand, with a son to the right and left of him, to receive the thousand guests who filed in through three entrances. In no time at all, the Night became Arabian—rajahs and sultans rivalling each other in the splendour of their retinues. Irving on these occasions was master of everything and everyone but himself. He was never quite able to assume an impersonal formality. As he grasped the hand of a ranee, he would catch sight of an old actor he had known in Manchester and, breaking the ranks, would single him out for a greeting of unceremonious warmth. In order to keep him, as it were, on the saluting base, Lord Aberdeen and the Premier of New Zealand assumed the duties of bodyguard and prevented him straying from his post.

When the last of that great assembly, probably the most remarkable that up to that time had ever assembled under any one roof in London, had drifted away, and the detectives and the caterers had departed, Irving, his sons, Austin and Bram Stoker were left alone in the crimson void. They all knew that the days of the Lyceum's glory were numbered and that "the sun-lit clearing in the dark forest" would echo no more to the light clapping of the chief's hands and to his quiet command—"Very good—yes—yes—begin the piece!" as the company settled down to rehearsal. It was six in the morning when, as they prepared to leave, Irving pronounced his verdict on his own genius: "I am going to say something I have never said before. I know none of you will misunderstand me. Looking back on my life's work and attempting—in all humility —to appraise it—I feel certain of one thing—mine is the only great Shylock."

The season ended on 19th July, with a matinee of *The Merchant of Venice*. For the last time Irving led Ellen Terry forward by the hand to acknowledge the applause of a Lyceum audience. The eyes of the public's "respectful, loyal and loving servant" were glistening with tears. He knew that their partnership was nearing its end; if the Lyceum had to perish, it was as well that it should not survive their parting. She was no less moved. "I shall never be in this theatre again, she said to him after their last curtain call: "I feel it…know it." The audience filed out, happily ignorant of the deeper significance of the occasion.

That afternoon, Irving made his final exit from the theatre that he had first entered so confidently thirty-one years before.

It was after giving a performance of *Becket*, in 1905, that he died in the lobby of a Bradford hotel. Thousands mourned him, but he also left behind plenty of critics. He rejected Shaw, he hated Ibsen, and he made Ellen Terry play only the roles that he wanted. He preferred costume drama because it allowed him to disguise his worst features…his legs. His company toured eight times playing in most major cities, a total of two hundred and nine weeks.

In London—

There's the Ivy, the Savoy and the divine
    Caprice
Where actors have all consumed a theatrical
    feast.
Larry and Vivien were always there
As were Binkie, Bunny and Bobby, and now
    they have Blair.
Though the food's very nice at Orsino's
It isn't a patch on Quaglino's
Let's not even refer to old Gino's!

Travel, they say, broadens the mind,
The food one discovers is often sublime.
From sushi to crab-cakes served up by
Charlie
But why, when you're in Sydney
It's always "shrimp on a barbie"?
Australians have such wonderful lamb
It's a pity, of course, that Dame Edna's a ham.
In Turkey the lamb is skewered, then set
    alight,
Their brandy is better than their mushy
    delight.

In Sweden the vegetables are all rather
    sodden.
In contrast, take Bergman whose plots were
    too modern.
Belgium is dramatic and fears an apocalypse
Which is a shame, considering their
    chocolates.

Theatres and Restaurants are so much alike
Your palette is satisfied by their works of
    art.
But Cooks and Playwrights will serve you
    a feast
Full of drama about man and beast.
Heaven and hell and some goulash too
Can lead to dyspepsia and often the loo.
But chicken and poultry are always a hit
Hey, wait a minute—don't rush it
Be like Pinter—take a pause—for a bit.

Ice cream and trifle will come much later
Served by an actor, who's your favourite
    waiter.

copyright E Sharland

CHAPTER THREE

Up the Years from Bloomsbury

George Arliss, the legendary actor of the 1920s, in his autobiography called *Up from Bloomsbury*, describes his love for the district of Bloomsbury:

"If anyone can tell me of a more highly respectable neighbourhood than Bloomsbury, London, W.C., England, about 1880, I should like to hear of it. Not that I have any use for it; I am not seeking such a spot in which to pass my declining years; but I do not believe it exists, and I will go so far as to defy any one to produce it. But if Bloomsbury, W.C., was respectable, what about Museum Street, Bloomsbury, W.C., with Mudie's Library at one end and the British Museum at the other! Could any street have its morals more securely guarded?

"Of course there were some shops in Museum Street, but what respectable shops! The stationer's opposite (Mr Hickman's), filled with all the things that industrious people need—ruled paper and steel pens, some photographs of Greek statues (the originals of which are to be seen in the British Museum), Guides to London, nice red blotting-paper—all looking so restful and good. And farther along, Mr. Stubbs', the bookseller's, kept by old Mr. Stubbs and young Mr. Stubbs. When you entered Mr. Stubbs' shop you knew at once you were in the Holy of Holies: in the half light you saw nothing distinctly, but by degrees you became conscious of the presence of Old Mr. Stubbs and Young Mr. Stubbs in soundless shoes, approaching you over a soundless floor. Old Mr. Stubbs with white whiskers, Young Mr. Stubbs with black. I am sure that if any one asked for any literature lighter than Homer's *Iliad* or Gibbon's *Decline and Fall* he was coldly and firmly bowed out by the two Mr. Stubbs.

"Then there was Mr. Parr at the corner shop. Mr. Parr had a long white beard, and at once suggested the twelve apostles. He sold cough drops—good old established cough drops that had the unmistakable odor and flavor of doing you good about them. I am sure they helped to give a smell of venerable respectability to the British Museum.

"But if this is Museum Street on a weekday, what is it on a Sunday? It is the aisle of a cathedral. Its respectability acts upon you like a narcotic. It is as ostentatiously respectable as a shiny Bible in the center of a round table. Nothing stirs till the bells of St. George's Church ring out; then if you peep from behind the drawing-room curtains you may see Mr. Parr walking steadfastly along the pavement, prayer book in hand, answering the call. No cough drops are sold on Sunday. It must be confessed that as an apostle he is rather spoilt by his top hat and his gloves; his gloves are too dark, and his boots are too shiny, for an apostle. But he typifies Museum Street on Sunday. Other worshippers follow in the wake of Mr. Parr."

Even though George Arliss became one of the most famous actors of his generation, he experienced the usual struggles of an actor trying to find work at the start of his career. From Bloomsbury he finds he has to search for work in Covent Garden. In one chapter of his book, called *The Weary Round of Agents*, he writes:

"I believe the out-of-work actor in England today frequents the district of Charing Cross Road and Shaftesbury Avenue, leading up to Piccadilly Circus. But in those days it was always the Strand. Having been to the agents, he crawled along the Strand from Wellington Street where stood (and still stands) the Lyceum Theatre in which Henry Irving and Ellen Terry were then playing—both in their prime, the unchallenged leaders of the English Stage; he crawled along the Strand to Bedford Street, always hoping to hear news that might lead to an engagement. Down Bedford Street on one side, up Bedford Street on the other, across the road and down the Strand on the opposite side of the way as far as Waterloo Bridge, which is opposite Wellington Street; cross the road, and up the Strand again from Wellington Street.

"There were houses of call—public-houses—between Bedford and Wellington Streets, frequented almost exclusively by people connected with the theatre. First "The Wellington" at the corner; a little farther the "Marble Halls"—the name given by the actors to the Adelphi bar in appreciation of its somewhat pretentious architecture—then the "Bodega" in Bedford Street; and on the other side of the Strand there was "Miss Barnes'." There was also Romano's, but this was reserved for the more opulent actor. In these public-houses might be met the actor who was in work and who seldom refused to relieve the distressful thirst of his less successful associates; although, to be just to my own profession, I record with satisfaction that the majority of actors who went into these saloons did not frequent them because they wanted drink, but solely for the purpose of seeking work. I don't know any class of society more industrious than the actor if he is given the opportunity of plying his trade. All he wants to do is to act—to work. And he is willing to work hard—much harder than the "working man". The more he has to do, the better he likes it, and the happier he is. That is my experience of the profession.

"But the actor out of work is a depressed and desolate fellow. And he has reason to be. What is his position? It is quite unlike that of the man who makes a specific thing and can give ocular demonstration that he makes it well. He has not the advantage of the painter who can show his work and be judged on the spot. The ability of the majority of the great unemployed in the theatre is entirely unknown to managers. The actor who faces a manager or an author knows that first of all his general appearance must suggest the part for which he is applying; and because he can show evidence that he has successfully played such and such parts, that doesn't prove that he can be relied upon for this one. Has he sufficient sense of comedy for the first act? Will he have the necessary repose for Act II? Can he carry that tragic moment in the third? Nobody can say. It is all a toss-up whether he gets the part or not and in most cases the decision is against him. Pity the poor actor who is out of work! He must try to look bright and cheerful and prosperous, no matter how often he is attacked by the pangs of hunger.

"There is much that is pitiful in the actor's life. What can be more pathetic than the "juvenile" actor who is getting old! The desperate effort to maintain his youth—the touching up of the hair that is beginning to go—or worse still, the terrible toupee when the hair has gone; the pulling in of the waistcoat to disguise the slipping chest; the jaunty air, no longer springing fresh and spontaneous to the fore, but dragged out for duty when it should be peacefully sleeping.

"And what of the women? They depend upon their physical attraction far more than the men. If a woman looks the part exactly, directors will often take a chance on her ability to act it. Can you wonder at actresses coming out "looking like the devil" in their anxiety to look beautiful and secure the part. They know that they must "strike twelve" as they walk into the manager's office; and so often in their eagerness they go a trifle too far and they only strike one. It is pathetic.

"I remember a young friend of mine, a quiet, pretty, dark girl, leaving a director's office in the depth of disappointment; she had failed to get a part for which she was capable but she was told she didn't look it. She suddenly got an idea: she hurried home, put on a fair wig and a picture hat, raced back to the office, sent another name, and blew in as a dashing blonde and got the part on her appearance alone.

"Of course, when actors and actresses become known, conditions for them are likely to be entirely different—but then how many in the crowded ranks become known!

"It must not be supposed that managers and casting directors are stony-hearted creatures who turn actors away and are entirely unconscious of the pain they are inflicting. On the contrary, more often than not they are most sympathetic; I know a number of them who would give much to be relieved of this undesirable duty.

Like many actors, George Arliss tried his hand at play-writing:

"I wrote a farce which I called *There and Back*. It was never a spectacular success, and the only remarkable thing about it was that it was accepted by the first manager to whom I read it and that it ran in some form or another for nearly fifteen years almost without a break.

"Charles Hawtrey and Arthur Williams played the leading parts. Hawtrey's part was afterwards taken up by Robert Loraine. The Shuberts bought it for America and it was produced at the old Princess Theatre with Charles E. Evans and Charles Hopper as the stars. My wife played in this production and scored a decided success. Later it became a musical play under the title of *I Loved a Lassie*, and later it returned to its original form of a one-act farce and was toured for many years by Charles E. Evans and his wife Helena Phillips under the name of *It's Up to You, William*. In this form it was still running in England when the Great War broke out and since then it has been done only spasmodically. It will probably be played many times in the future; for the central idea is funny and capable of being written up every ten years or so.

To the Lady Behind Me at the Theatre

Dear madam, you have seen this play;
I never saw it till today,
You know the details of the plot,
But, let me tell you, I do not.
The author seeks to keep from me
The murderer's identity.
And you are not a friend of his
If you keep shouting who it is.
The actors in their funny way
Have several funny things to say,
But they do not amuse me more
If you have said them just before;
The merit of the drama lies,
I understand, in some surprise;
But the surprise must now be small
Since you have just foretold it all.
The lady you have brought with you
Is, I infer, a half-wit too,
But I can understand the piece
Without assistance from your niece.

In short, foul woman, it would suit
Me just as well if you were mute,
In fact, to make my meaning plain,
I trust you will not speak again.
And may I add one human touch?
Don't breathe upon my neck so much.

A P Herbert

CHAPTER FOUR

James Agate 1877–1947

"If all the people represented by the characters in the plays of Messrs. Coward, Lonsdale, Arlen and Company were put into a bag and drowned in the Thames the intellectual and industrial, artistic and social world of London would not be one whit the poorer."

London theatre critic and grand bon vivant, James Agate was well known for his taste in wine at the restaurants featured in this book. He began writing for the *Manchester Guardian*, then in *The Sunday Times* in 1923. As his notoriety grew he became over-conscious of his own personality. He wrote his nine-volume selection from his diary *Ego 1932–1947* and a biography of Rachel, the great French actress, also twenty volumes of his essays and reviews.

Martin Banham writes:

> His natural conservatism was a discouragement to dramatic innovation, and his delight in flamboyant actors, from Sarah Bernhardt to Donald Wolfit, however stylishly expressed, was perilously nostalgic.

In his 1926 book *A Short View of the English Stage*, Agate described the situation at that time as follows:

> "A large part of the London theatre is given up to plays about dope fiends and jazz-maniacs; other large tracts are abandoned to the inanities of musical comedy. Roughly speaking, three-fourths of the London stage is closed to persons possessed of the slightest particle of intellect or the least feeling for the drama.

and:

> It is useless to tell the begetters of these characters that they are not of use; one wonders whether they can be made to see that they are not polite, and that the world they move in is ill-bred. Yet I feel sure that this wave of vulgarity will pass.

It has already deleted the West-End theatre from among those things in which any rational person can take interest. Always, of course, with exceptions. And it is a commonplace that these plays hold no interest for the millions outside what Sir Arthur Pinero used to call "our little parish of St. James's".

The Critic

The critic of the morning Press
Devotes his day to idleness;
But then he has to sit and write
His notice very late at night,
When he would so much rather be
Tucked up in bed like you and me.
No wonder he's a trifle sharp
And shows a tendency to carp.

Captious and cross the critic creeps
Exhausted into bed and sleeps.
Rising next day in buoyant mood
He feels once more that life is good;
Springs out of bed and cuts a caper
And asks to see the morning paper.
His cheeks turn pale; his eyes grow wet;
He's filled with infinite regret,
As he peruses in the light
The brutal things he wrote last night.

Guy Boas (1925)

The cook was a good cook, as cooks go, and as good cooks go, she went.
Saki

Most dear actors, eat no onions or garlic, for we are to utter sweet breath.
Shakespeare, *A Midsummer Night's Dream*

15

CHAPTER FIVE

Historic London Theatrical Restaurants

When you walk in the footsteps of Garrick, Irving, Kean, Ellen Terry around Covent Garden, somehow you will find that their spirits will enter your bones. Spend time finding the great restaurants they frequented and revive their memory. For the first time, places of theatrical interest are included which you won't be able to find on street maps or Theatre What's On brochures.

RULES, 35 Maiden Lane—off Southampton Street, Covent Garden

Throughout its long history the tables of Rules have been crowded with writers, artists, lawyers, journalists and actors. As well as being frequented by great literary talents— including Charles Dickens, William Makepeace Thackeray, John Galsworthy and H G Wells—Rules has also appeared in novels by Rosamond Lehmann, Evelyn Waugh, Graham Greene, John Le Carré, Dick Francis, Penelope Lively and Claire Rayner.

The actors and actresses who have passed through Rules are legion. Down the decades Rules has been an unofficial "Green Room" for the world of entertainment from Henry Irving to Laurence Olivier, and the history of the English stage adorns the walls. The sibling art of the cinema has contributed its own distinguished list of names including Buster Keaton, Charles Laughton, Clark Gable, Charlie Chaplin and John Barrymore.

The past lives on at Rules and can be seen on the walls all around you—captured in literally hundreds of drawings, paintings and cartoons. The late John Betjeman, then Poet Laureate, described the ground floor interior as "unique and irreplaceable, and part of literary and theatrical London".

The King Edward Room, an intimate, velvet-swagged room on the first floor, by the lattice window, was once the most celebrated "Table for Two" in London. This was the Prince of Wales' favourite spot for wining and dining the beautiful actress, Lily Langtry. So frequent were his visits that Rules put in a special door to enable the prince to enter and leave without having to walk through the restaurant. Their signed portraits still hang on the walls.

The Charles Dickens Room, a private dining room, is named after the writer who has pride of place in the restaurant's private pantheon because his association with Rules was so poignant. As a young boy he often wandered hungry through the streets and alleys of Covent Garden, his wage from the blacking factory allowing him only a sniff of the mouth-watering aromas that rose from the kitchens. He never forgot those hard times, even when he could afford to enjoy the restaurant later in his life. Rules' memorabilia include playbills for performances of *Not So Bad As We Seem* and *Mr Nightingale's Diary*, which Dickens produced and performed in, and which he brought to the restaurant himself.

The Greene Room is of course named after Graham Greene, a voluntary exile from Britain who spent much of his life in the South of France, but who still chose to spend all his birthdays in the quintessentially British surroundings of Rules. He was certain to visit the restaurant whenever he returned to London, and it features in several of his books including *The End of the Affair*. Letters from Greene and his sister Elizabeth are displayed on the walls of the Greene Room, bearing witness to Rules' long and happy association with the man widely considered to be Britain's greatest twentieth-century writer.

Rules serves the traditional food of this country at its best. It specialises in classic game cookery, oysters, pies and puddings. Rules is fortunate in owning an estate in the High Pennines, "England's last wilderness", which supplies game for the restaurant. Reservations are essential; phone 0207-836-5314.

THE IVY—*West Street, off Cambridge Circus*

A well-known eating place for theatre/media/publishing people. It has a long history of association with famous stars of the 'twenties and 'thirties. Mario Gallati, the head waiter, was a friend of Noel Coward and Ivor Novello. Throughout the twenties he became friends with Gertie Lawrence, Bea Lillie, Winston Churchill, Pavlova, and Dame Marie Tempest. He then started his own restaurant, the Caprice in Arlington Street, just down from the Ritz in 1947. His book, *Gallati at the Caprice,* is full of anecdotes about famous people and what they ate, life at the Ivy, followed by life at the Caprice.

When Noel Coward was first trying to interest producers in his work, he began lunching regularly at the Ivy. He could ill afford it and the owner was kind enough to allow him credit. They became great friends. He describes a particular occasion, not apparently untypical, in 1927, when he had two flops in the same year. The first was *Home Chat* followed almost immediately by *Sirocco* which was an absolute disaster. He was sitting in the stalls with his mother on the first night of *Sirocco* and was painfully aware of the reaction of the audience, who was unsympathetic, to say the least. The audience laughed and booed throughout the play and afterwards, at the stage door, the crowd insulted him and some even spat at him, to the point that he wrote that he had to send out his jacket to be cleaned the next day. Even his mother, who was usually unaware of any difficulties, sensed that the play was not being well received. They had had dinner at the Ivy before the performance without any intimation of what was going to happen.

The next day the reviews were so bad that Coward contemplated leaving the city or even the country until the storm blew over; however he decided to brazen it out. He went for as usual to the Ivy for lunch the next day.

He sat at his usual table, not sure of what to expect. However, the atmosphere was friendly and quietly sympathetic; he commented that no actors or actresses came over to revile him and the maitre d' in a rare gesture gave him two drinks on the house.

When you go to the Ivy, they will point out his table inside the door.

LE CAPRICE in Arlington Street

Le Caprice in Arlington Street was opened by Mario Gallati in 1947 when he had retired from the Ivy. Many of his friends, including Ivor Novello, helped him financially to open his own restaurant. It is still the fashionable place to be seen in. In his book, Mario recounts many stories and anecdotes. One lunchtime, sitting along the wall at different tables were Orson Welles, Robert Morley, Wolf Mankowitz, the late Oliver Hardy of Laurel and Hardy fame, and portly Henry Sherek, quite an impressive sight. Orson Welles is reputed to have called over to Mario and said, "Mario, whatever else you may say, THIS side of the restaurant is a fine advertisement for Caprice food." Whenever Charlie Chaplin came to London Mario knew he would dine at the Caprice as the former had known Mario ever since he had started out as a waiter at Romano's. Coward liked to order aiolis (mayonnaise with juice of garlic). He would please Coward enormously with a bowl of bouillabaisse with aiolis served in the middle of it.

Mario's book is full of famous names from Pablo Picasso to Maria Callas at the Caprice. His chapter on what they all ate is interesting, including all their favourite dishes and requests. Maria Callas always started with caviar followed by a small steak with lots of green salad and green vegetables.

Terence Rattigan liked steak and kidney pudding for lunch and was also very keen on plovers' eggs.

Clients may be surprised to know that the kitchens of the Caprice are larger than the restaurant itself. This, of course, is at it should be, for the kitchens of a first-class restaurant are a real world below stairs.

THE GRILL ROOM at the CAFE ROYAL in Regent Street

This, just north of Piccadilly Circus is, according to the late Cecil Beaton, the most beautiful dining room in London. Unfortunately the famous brasserie has now closed and a new owner has converted it into a "Cheers" bar. However, the Grill Room is still in business. With gilt-edged mirrors, crystal and red velvet, it conjures up the Edwardian elegance with a French touch. Sir Herbert Tree once commented, "If you want to see English people at their most English, go to the Cafe Royal where they are trying their hardest to be French."

It was in the brasserie that poets, painters, wits and eccentrics gathered. Here Oscar Wilde held court night after night, arguing into the small hours with, among others, Aubrey Beardsley, Frank Harris and Bernard Shaw. In November 1922, the somewhat startling announcement was made that the Cafe Royal was to be pulled down and rebuilt. "They might as well have told us," wrote Y W H Crossland, "that the British Empire is to be pulled down and redecorated." Charles Forte bought the Cafe Royal in 1954 and refurbished and extended it into the eight-storey conference and banqueting facility that stands in Regent Street today. The Grill Room is a "must".

THE CRITERION BRASSERIE

(Marco Pierre White)—Criterion Restaurant in Piccadilly

The Criterion Brasserie, in the heart of Piccadilly Circus, is owned by celebrated chef Marco Pierre White, the youngest chef, and the first Englishman, ever to be awarded three "Michelin Stars". The menu is predominantly French with Mediterranean influences and allows exceptional food to be enjoyed in captivating surroundings.

Piccadilly (London's Magic Mile) derives its name from the pickadill, a type of support which gave the distinctive tilt to the Elizabethan ruff. Robert Baker, a seventeenth-century draper, made so much money from pickadills that he built a great house for himself on the site of what is now Great Windmill Street.

Although it is hard to imagine today, Piccadilly was still a country lane as late as 1633. Reference to this was given in Gerard's herbal, saying that "The small wild buglosse grows upon the drie ditch banks of Pickadilla". The site of the Criterion restaurant has been dispensing hospitality for hundreds of years. In 1685 it was occupied in part by the White Bear Inn, an important coach terminus and the St James's Market. In 1674 the non-conformist preacher Richard Baxter gave his first sermon in the upstairs rooms of the market building. It was said that the main floor beam cracked under the weight of the audience.

The Criterion restaurant and theatre were constructed within the one building in 1873, to the designs of Thomas Verity, for the well-known wine merchants and railway caterers Spiers and Pond. Writing in 1890, Old and New London described it as a handsome building which combined under the one roof the advantages of a restaurant on an unusually large scale with reading, billiards and hairdressing rooms, a cigar divan, a concert hall, ballroom and theatre.

The cost of this huge project was initially estimated at £25,000 but quickly grew to over £80,000 (about £8,000,000 in today's money). No expense was spared. Verity designed the ground floor to house the vestibule, dining rooms and smoking rooms. The first floor was devoted to dining and serving rooms, the second floor was occupied by the Grand Hall with a picture gallery and a "Ball supper room" both on the Jermyn St side. The entire building has been modified through the years with the restaurant also seeing many additions over time. However, the building remains the finest work of Verity who is considered one of the leading theatre architects of his day.

During its long life the Criterion Restaurant has been a variety of restaurants, dining rooms and tea-rooms. During the London Blitz, the Criterion was fitted with false walls and ceilings to protect the ornate interior. Post-war, the Criterion became the twenty-four-hour Boots Chemist, and was eventually restored to its former glory by Rocco Forte at the end of the 1980s, the highlight being the amazing re-discovery of its beautiful walls and ceiling, hidden for over forty years.

The Criterion Brasserie was re-opened by Marco Pierre White in 1995 breathing new life into London's only neo-byzantine restaurant. The grand entrance, flanked by potted palms leads to a vast bar topped with ornate drum lamps. The restaurant itself features ornate marble walls with a glittering gold mosaic ceiling designed to evoke images of Arabian nights.

So you can plan a romantic dinner for two or invite 300 guests to the party to end all parties! One of these parties was given for Sir John Gielgud in 1992 after the world premiere in the Criterion Theatre next door of the film *Swansong* directed by Kenneth Branagh. "The film is a brief but brilliant dialogue about life, love and the theatre," explained Branagh at the Criterion Brasserie's party later. He was joined for a cake-cutting ceremony by Sally Green, actor Sir Ian McKellen and John Sessions. Most of the London theatre world was there, and there was music and dancing till the early hours. It was one of the most memorable theatre parties in the West End, with Sir John Gielgud receiving a standing ovation after the film.

SIMPSON'S-IN-THE-STRAND

A Brief History

Early in the nineteenth century, 101/102 Strand was occupied by the Reis family who had settled in London from Portugal. Previously this site had been famous for the "Fountain Tavern" and the home of the "Kit Kat Club"—a literary group of such well-known individuals as Dr Samuel Johnson, Congreve, Lamb, Sir Hugh Walpole.

In 1828 Samuel Reis decided to open the ground floor as a Cigar Divan. Gentlemen, for a fee of one guinea a year or 1/6d a day, could sit in comfortable "Divans", drink coffee, smoke cigars, read papers or play chess (see the poster outside the gentlemen's cloakroom on the first floor).

During this period, chess became very popular with the emerging middle classes and the Divan became the favourite place for the chess public to meet and even meet the contestants. This was greatly helped by Samuel Reis who became personally involved with the players and in the promotion of chess. In 1836, Reis provided them with temporary accommodation at his home above the Divan. In 1840, Reis also tried to help the French player La Bourdonnais who was having serious problems with ill-health and a lack of funds by bringing him over from Paris to be the professional at the Divan. After only two days of playing in front of large crowds, La Bourdonnais' illness became too serious for him to continue and within a few weeks he had died.

In 1843, Howard Staunton, a regular at the Divan, beat the acknowledged world champion Pierre Fournier de Saint-Amant in Paris (the last game took fourteen hours to play). This completely unexpected result caused an explosion of enthusiasm for chess in England. London became the premier city in world chess and the "Grand Divan" replaced the Cafe de la Regence in Paris as the Mecca for ambitious chess players.

At this time, Samuel Reis was also concentrating on improving the commercial potential of the Divan. In 1848, Samuel Reis brought in John Simpson to enlarge the space of the ground floor and improve the catering facilities. Simpson employed the noted chef from the Reform Club—Alexis Soyer. He also introduced the practice of wheeling large joints of meat on silver-domed trolleys to the tables and carving them there. The name was changed to Simpson's Grand Divan and Tavern and the chess players were moved to their own "magnificent saloon" on the second floor (where the Regency Room is now) with its own entrance from the street.

In 1849, this new saloon played host to the first-ever recorded chess tournament and two years later, the first international tournament, organised by Staunton, to coincide with the Great Exhibition held in Hyde Park.

In 1862, the restaurant was sold to Edmund Cathie. Cathie was a complete anglophile. He insisted that everything was British and replaced terms such as "Menu" with "Bill of Fare" and "Maitre D'Hotel" with "Superintendent". This policy succeeded in enhancing Simpson's business, the result of which saw Simpson's closing for the first time in 1866 in order to allow Cathie to enlarge the eating areas. The chess saloon was altered to a ladies' dining room and a smaller chess room was created at the front of the building.

In 1898, Cathie sold the restaurant to Richard D'Oyley Carte who had built the Savoy Hotel next door and so it became part of the Savoy Group.

With ever greater traffic demands on the Strand, it was agreed that the road would have to be widened, and so on Saturday, 14th February 1903 Simpson's was closed for only the second time in its history, and demolished to make way for the building we now occupy. Work took just over a year and the restaurant re-opened in May 1904 as Simpson's-in-the-Strand. A new dining room was introduced on the first floor overlooking the Strand, known as the West Room, where men and women were allowed to dine together. A small chess room was provided, but failed to become established and fell into disuse.

Scott ate his last meal here before departing for the Antarctic. The literary connections are numerous, from Charles Dickens, Anthony Trollope, and P G Wodehouse to, more recently, Sir Kingsley Amis and P D James. For all its fabled past, Simpson's-in-the-Strand lives in the present.

THE SAVOY

The Savoy Hotel—Did you know?—

1 In 1246, Count Peter of Savoy was given the land between the Strand and the Thames by King Henry III for an annual rent of three barbed arrows. Here Count Peter built The Palace of Savoy, hailed as "the fayrest mannor in Europe". This subsequently became the residence of John of Gaunt, Duke of Lancaster. The Palace of Savoy was destroyed in 1381.

2 In 1884, the construction of the Savoy began using the profits of the Savoy Theatre. James McNeill Whistler sketched the scaffolding, returning in May 1896 to stay at the property. His subsequent series of inspired etchings made from his Savoy window captured the essence of London at the close of the century.

3 On 6th August, 1889 the Savoy opened with single rooms costing 7s 6d (37 1/2p) per day and double rooms 12s (60p). An American, Harry Rosenfeld from Chicago, used the first sovereign to pay for a bottle of Moet et Chandon champagne at the Savoy. The coin is still kept in the hotel safe.

4 Claude Monet's passion for the Thames led him to paint it in all-weather conditions and times of the day—but almost always from the same vantage point—his room on the fifth floor of the Savoy. When the light changed, he would put one canvas aside and turn his attention to another, and so on as the day advanced. He stayed at the hotel on three occasions between 1899 and 1901. Waterloo Bridge painted in 1900 is now in Dublin.

5 Just before leaving for South Africa early in 1898, businessman Joel Wolff gave a dinner party for fourteen at the hotel. One guest cancelled at the last minute but the host balked at the superstition that whoever left the table earliest would be destined to die first. A few weeks later, Woolff was shot dead in his office in Johannesburg. Since then, if there happened

to be thirteen guests at a party, a member of staff would be recruited to join them. This, however, was not always convenient or practical so Kaspar the cat was commissioned by the Savoy from art-deco designer Basil Ionides in 1926. His brief was to design a three-foot-high cat, which he carved from a single piece of plane tree.

Christened Kaspar, he now lives on a high shelf in the Pinafore Room with his back to a mirror and is only removed if a party of thirteen is lunching or dining at the Savoy. He is then placed on the fourteenth chair with a napkin tied around his neck and is treated as a bona fide guest, the place settings before him changed as he is served each course of the meal.

---

6 Savoy Court, leading to the Strand entrance of the Savoy, is the first and only road in Britain down which traffic travels on the right hand side.

---

7 The Duc D'Orleans, claimant to the French throne, was the first guest for whom the Savoy obligingly stamped the fleur-de-lis crest on the crockery and linen he used.

---

8 The first "water party" in 1905 was also the hotel's most elaborate, known as the famous Gondola Dinner. Host George Kessler, a Wall Street financier, entertained his guests in a recreated Venice. The courtyard was made watertight and flooded to a depth of four feet, scenery erected around the walls, gondolas built, costumes designed and guests dined in gondolas on the Grand Canal. Caruso was there as a singing gondolier.

---

9 A member of the Strauss family was the first artist hired by the Savoy to provide music while guests dined. The idea, said Ritz, was to "cover the silence which hangs like a pall over an English dining table".

---

10 The Savoy was the site of the first verbal altercation between Lord Queensbury and Oscar Wilde.

---

11 29th May, 1913—Tradition was overturned when two diners at the Savoy got up to dance to the string orchestra. As others followed suit, a space was cleared between the tables and social tradition was overturned. Dining to music was not new, however dining and dancing had always been entirely separate activities. Over the next four decades, the Savoy became established for dinner-dancing.

---

12 Pêches Melba was originally dreamed up by Escoffier to finish a dinner celebrating Dame Nellie Melba's performance as Elsa in *Lohengrin*. Melba Toast was also named in honour of Dame Nellie, although in this case, devised by Madame Ritz with Escoffier.

---

13 The Pilgrim's Society of Great Britain was formed at the Savoy in 1902 on the eve of King Edward's coronation by Sir William Goode and his American friends, George Wilson and Lindsay Russell. They decided to form a club "composed of Americans like ourselves, who have made the pilgrimage over here and have received and appreciated British hospitality and there will be English members who have made the pilgrimage and discovered that we are not all Red Indians". Soon after, a sister society, The Pilgrims of the United States, was formed.

———

14 One of the most distinguished dishwashers to have graced the Savoy's kitchens was Guccio Gucci. As a young Italian in London at the turn of the century, he was so impressed with the glamour and wealth of the guests that he returned to Florence and started his renowned luxury leather goods company.

———

15 Omelette Arnold Bennett, named after novelist Arnold Bennett, who immortalised the inner sanctum of the Savoy management in his novel, *The Imperial Palace*, was actually invented by the author himself and is still served in the Savoy Grill today.

———

16 Austrian opera singer, Richard Tauber, signed his first contract to sing in England on the back of a Savoy restaurant menu.

———

17 Guglielmo Marconi made the first wireless broadcast to the United States from the Savoy.

———

18 The two Savoy bands, Bert Ralton and his Havana Band and the Savoy Orpheans, were the first to broadcast regularly from any hotel.

———

19 George Gershwin gave *Rhapsody in Blue* its first English premiere at the Savoy.

———

20 Silent-screen heart-throb George Galli disappeared mysteriously after checking out of the Savoy and was found thirty-five years later, having joined a Belgian Monastery.

———

21 "Charleston Blues", a new dance in foxtrot tempo was publicly demonstrated for the first time in England by Mr and Mrs Victor Silvester in the ballroom.

———

22 The first rider in the Savoy ballroom was silent film star cowboy Tom Mix and his famous steed, Tony, who made a surprise appearance at a banquet in their honour.

———

23 The first fireproof eiderdown was provided for actor Lionel Barrymore, who had a habit of reading in bed while he chain-smoked.

24 The Russian prima ballerina Anna Pavlova first danced in cabaret at the Savoy.

25 Rudolph Valentino's first public appearances at the Savoy were when he danced at the thé dansant afternoons.

26 During the Second World War, when a bomb which fell on the Strand knocked down the leader of the Savoy's dance band, Noel Coward stepped to the piano and soothed spirits by singing his own compositions.

27 The hotel was hit twice in one night by high explosive bombs believed to be aimed at Waterloo Station. The ARP men would come out and sweep firebombs off the roof. The one that blew out the entire riverside front of the Savoy was a landmine—it came down on a parachute and landed in a tree outside. Despite these attacks, the Savoy never once closed its doors and learnt after the war that the hotel was one of ten top targets for the Luftwaffe.

28 Film star Elizabeth Taylor spent her honeymoon with first husband Nicky Hilton in a suite at the Savoy.

29 Sir Laurence Olivier and Vivien Leigh first laid eyes on each other at the Savoy.

32 In a gesture unheard of in Royal Family archives, the Queen Mother stood to applaud Maria Callas when she arrived at the Savoy after a triumphant opening in *Tosca*.

33 The first wild animal to be brought to a party at the Savoy was Billy Butlin's pet leopard who came for a cocktail party to celebrate Smart's circus.

34 The Savoy hosted the first night party for Rogers and Hammerstein's *South Pacific*.

35 The Savoy hosted the launch ball for the epic film, *Cleopatra,* starring Elizabeth Taylor and Richard Burton.

36 The first restaurant guests to order porridge and pea sandwiches were John, Paul, George and Ringo aka The Beatles when they came to call on Bob Dylan in 1965.

37 *Ready Steady Go* hostess, Cathy McGowann was asked to leave the Savoy when she turned up in a trouser suit. In 1967, actress Geraldine Chaplin was also refused admission to dine when she turned up in a suit by Pierre Cardin. A trouser-clad Twiggy retired to the ladies room to change into a miniskirt and was allowed to stay. By 1969, this rule was relaxed.

---

38 Bob Dylan stayed at the Savoy and was refused entrance to the restaurants as he never wore a tie.

---

39. The day after fifteen-year-old musical comedy star Tommy Steele left school, his mother took him to the Savoy hoping he would get a job as a pageboy. Tommy took one look at the white gloves and decided to sail to New York the next day. He was later to have his wedding reception at the Savoy.

---

40 The first celebrity flood at the Savoy happened when Elton John let his bath overflow.

---

41 During the Second World War, American war correspondents spent a lot of time at the Savoy. Titch's Bar became their unofficial headquarters and they remained steadfast clients of the hotel, even after fifty rooms were damaged by a bomb. A government minister was overheard complaining that England's shortage of whisky could be directly attributed to the habits of these foreign journalists!

---

42 When the Second World War's blackout ended in 1945, the Savoy was the first public building to switch on its lights.

---

43 A letter from Czechoslovakia addressed "To The Manager of The Greatest Hotel in London" was forwarded by the Post Office with the remark—try Savoy Hotel, WC2.

---

44 In 1953, HM Queen Elizabeth II's Coronation Ball was held at the Savoy.

---

45 Approximately 3,000 private luncheons, dinners and receptions are held at the Savoy during an average year.

---

46 The Savoy operates its own private electricity generating system—Strand Power Co— supporting all lifts and services in an emergency.

---

47 The Savoy was the first hotel to establish a hotel management training scheme. "Trained at the Savoy" has become a byword for quality in the industry. Many of the students were

given continental experience for a year before returning to home duties. Others were given the opportunity to attend courses at technical college.

---

48 Eight china patterns are used at the Savoy with Wedgwood for room service, Royal Doulton in the restaurant; Worcester in the Gilbert & Sullivan rooms, featuring characters from the operas. Different designs are used for the Grill, Banqueting, Floor Service and the Upstairs Bar. Currently, over 230,000 pieces of china and glass are in use with nine months supply reserve stock. All are made exclusively to the Savoy's own design.

---

49 The annual consumption of foodstuffs at the Savoy is as follows, unless otherwise stated:

Caviar 160 kg
Smoked Salmon 9,500 sides
Foie gras 1,000 lb
Oysters 52,000
Eggs 6,000,000
Milk 45,000 gallons

Smaller Theatre Restaurants

You might like to have a drink or a meal before or after the theatre at a restaurant associated with theatre personalities, where actors and other theatricals congregate. Among them are:

J SHEEKEY

A fish restaurant at 28 St Martin's Court, which opened in 1896 with just an oyster stall. Sheekey, an Irishman, bought the four small shops next door and opened his restaurant. It became very popular with theatre people, and their signed photos line the walls of the five rooms. From theatre stars to Hollywood legends, they all seem to have dined here. When Sheekey died, his grand-daughter, Emmie Williams, carried on as proprietor.

Massive renovations took place in 1998, and the actress Googie Withers was the first person through the door when the restaurant reopened. The bar also serves a fish menu and is very busy before and after the theatre.

LUIGI'S

An Italian restaurant in Tavistock Street in Covent Garden where actors have been eating for the past forty years, especially members of the Royal Shakespeare Company when it was based at the Aldwych Theatre. The interior walls are crammed with autographed photos of actors and directors, as in Sheeky's.

JOE ALLEN'S

Also in Covent Garden, and a popular haunt for actors after the show. Drinks only with dinner.

THE SALISBURY

90 St Martins Lane, Covent Garden, London WC2 4AP

This pub's very name is part of the fabric of British history and reaches back to Robert Cecil, the first Earl of Salisbury and the wisest man in Tudor politics. It was his nineteenth-century descendant—the third Marquis of Salisbury, Queen Victoria's favourite prime minister—from whom the site of the tavern was originally leased in 1892. The Salisbury is possibly London's most magnificently preserved historic drinking house. With its original cut glass and hand-carved mahogany splendour it stands out in the heart of Theatreland. It is sometimes called the Actors' Pub because of its association with so many of the casts who play at nearby theatres.

Apologies for all the omissions, but there is very little information about the great actors and writers personal taste in food and restaurants, and therefore they are not included.

Beware of young women who love neither wine nor truffles nor cheese nor music.
Colette

We may live without friends, we may live without books, but civilized man cannot live without cooks.
Owen Meredith

CHAPTER SIX

George Bernard Shaw

Henrietta Street, which runs from Bedford Street to the south side of the Piazza in Covent Garden, holds a number of historic houses, yet there is a remarkable absence of the famous Blue Plaques of London. Although there is a plaque on the house in Fitzroy Square in Bloomsbury where both GBS and Virginia Wolf lived at different periods, one of the most important events in GBS's life took place in Henrietta Street.

He was married there to Charlotte Payne Townsend, and reports written say that the hastily recruited witness was mistaken by the registrar for the groom, and that GBS was so badly dressed that he was taken for a witness.

No doubt Charlotte Payne Townsend helped Shaw tremendously as a nurse, companion and wife. He had been suffering from an infected foot that was not healing since he tried to ignore it and kept walking around on his daily rounds without dressing it properly.

Charlotte had been his secretary, typing his manuscripts and helping with his massive workload of answering correspondence and proof-reading his speeches. When she visited him in Fitzroy Square she was appalled at his living conditions.

He worked in a very small room that was in a perpetual state of dirt and disorder. He kept the window wide open, day and night, winter and summer, and the dust and smut that entered thereby settled on books, furniture and papers, being scattered over a wider area whenever attempts were made to remove them. The mass of matter on the table was chaotic; heaps of letters, pages of manuscripts, books, envelopes, writing-paper, pens, butter, sugar, apples, knives, forks, spoons, sometimes a cup of cocoa or a half-finished plate of porridge, a saucepan, and all undusted, as his papers must not be touched. The table, the typewriter and the wood-railed chair in which he sat filled the room, forcing anyone who entered it to move sideways like a crab.

As he read books while he was dressing and undressing and deposited them, open, on the table without bothering to shut them, there was a fair state of chaos. His mother never came into the room, and they did not have their meals together. When his mother was in for a meal, the servant brought in a plateful of cooked eggs and put them down on the nearest pile of books or papers. He writes:

It was planned I must go away into the country the moment I could be moved, and that somebody must seriously take in hand the job of looking after me. Equally plain that Charlotte was the inevitable and predestined agent appointed by destiny.

I found that my own objection to my marriage has ceased with my objection to my own death.

Charlotte took a house for me to convalesce in, and in order to save her reputation I sent her out for a marriage licence and a ring.

He was hardly in a physical condition to go out and get them himself.

One of the subjects we discussed was money. I was not making enough money to support Charlotte in the manner to which she was accustomed, and if I left Fitzroy Square my mother would not be able to manage on the fees she earned from teaching music.

So Charlotte settled an annuity on his mother for life. When Shaw went back to Fitzroy Square after his wedding and broke the news to his mother she made no comment beyond saying that it was not unexpected. She supposed that she must call Miss Payne Townsend Charlotte now, though "Carlotta was rather more descriptive, she looked a Carlotta. She had taken to ouija boards and seances and had ideas on the unseen forces beyond the material world."

Charlotte went to pack up, and it was a relief to get back to Adelphi Terrace. Shaw worked all week in his apartment there and, after purchasing a house at Ayot St Lawrence, would drive there for the weekends. So Covent Garden was his closet "quartier" and no doubt he frequented Rules and the Savoy many times.

He entertained frequently in Adelphi Terrace, and there are many accounts from the writers of the day of how he would entertain his guests, often making an entrance through the double doors of the living room in a rather dramatic fashion and continuing to talk his guests into a corner over lunch.

The Apple Cart

George Bernard Shaw's plays were so successful in New York that he said Richard Mansfield made him a fortune that led to his subsequent success in London. In his play *The Apple Cart* Shaw suggests that America might like to re-join the British Empire. Here is a short extract from a scene involving a conversation between the King and Queen and the American Ambassador in London. The Ambassador is speaking:

VANHATTAN: Well, we find here everything we are accustomed to: our industrial products, our books, our plays, our sports, our Christian Science churches, our osteopaths, our movies and talkies. Put it in a small parcel and say our goods and our ideas. A political union with us will be just the official recognition of an already accomplished fact. A union of hearts, you might call it.

THE QUEEN: You forget, Mr Vanhattan. We have a great national tradition.

VANHATTAN: The United States, ma'am, have absorbed all the great national traditions, and blended them with their own glorious tradition of Freedom into something that is unique and universal.

THE QUEEN: We have a civilised culture which is peculiar to ourselves. It may not be better than yours: but it is different.

VANHATTAN: Well, is it? We found that culture enshrined in British material works of art; in the stately country homes of your nobility, in the cathedrals our common forefathers built as the country houses of God. What did you do with them? You sold them to us. I was brought up in the shade of Ely Cathedral, the removal of which from the county of Cambridge to New Jersey was my dear old father's first big professional job. The building which stands on its former site is a very fine one; in my opinion the best example of reinforced concrete of its period; but is was designed by an American architect, and built by the Synthetic Building Materials Trust, an international affair. Believe me, the English people, the real English people who take things as they come instead of reading books about them, will be more at home with us than they are with the old English notions which our tourists try to keep alive. When you find some country gentleman keeping up the old English customs at Christmas and so forth, who is he? An American who has bought the place. Your people get up the show for him because he pays for it, not because it is natural to them.

THE QUEEN (with a sigh): Our own best families go so much to Ireland nowadays. People should not be allowed to go from England to Ireland. They never come back.

VANHATTAN: Well, can you blame them, ma'am? Look at the climate!

THE QUEEN: No; it is not the climate. It is the Horse Show.

NARRATOR: The King rises very thoughtfully; and Vanhattan follows his example.

MAGNUS: I must think over this. I have known for years past that it was on the cards. When I was young, and under the influence of our family tradition, which of course never recognised the rebellion of the American colonies as valid, I actually dreamt of a reunited English-speaking empire at the head of civilisation.

VANHATTAN: Fine! Great! And now come true.

MAGNUS: Not yet. Now that I am older and wiser I find the reality less attractive than the dream.

VANHATTAN: And is that all I am to report to the President, sir? He will be disappointed. I am a little taken aback, myself.

MAGNUS: For the present, that is all. This may be a great idea—

VANHATTAN: Surely, surely.

MAGNUS: It may also be a trap in which England will perish.

VANHATTAN (encouragingly): Oh, I shouldn't look at it that way. Besides, nothing—not even dear old England—can last for ever. Progress, you know, sir, progress, progress!

MAGNUS: Just so, just so. We may survive only as another star on your flag. Still, we cling to the little scrap of individuality you have left us. If we must merge, as you call it—or did you say submerge?—some of us will swim to the last.

George Bernard returned to Britain and never looked back. His play *Pygmalion* was turned into *My Fair Lady*, and the rest is history.

> Some day, you'll eat a pork chop, Joey, and then God
> help all women.
> Mrs Patrick Campbell to Bernard Shaw

CHAPTER SEVEN

Sir John Gielgud

Rules was Sir John Gielgud's favourite London restaurant, and even though he dined there often when he was in town, towards the end of his life, he entertained mostly in his home. Between film work he would ask most people for lunch, rather than dinner, at his country house.

One of his biographers, John Miller, kindly gave me this report about his visits there.

John Gielgud at Home

I worked with John Gielgud over the last twenty-five years of his life, and visited him at his country home in Buckinghamshire on many occasions to discuss our next project for radio, television, or various books. He usually said, "Come about noon, and stay for lunch."

The pattern of the visit was invariably the same. His long-time companion, Martin Hensler, would come and unlock the garden gate and take me up the steps to the house, where Sir John was waiting in the hall. We walked through the small but elegant dining-room to the high-ceilinged Gallery Room, with the double staircase at the end leading up to the bookshelves. We sat and talked on the large sofas grouped around the fireplace, and Sir John would offer sherry as an aperitif.

Promptly at one o'clock Martin came and summoned us in to lunch. I would be offered wine to accompany my meal, but Sir John invariably just drank mineral water. He told me once that in his youth he used to love cocktails and champagne, and had such an appetite for oysters that he feared he must have seemed very greedy. But in his last three decades he became quite abstemious himself, whilst never stinting in the fare he offered his guests.

The two of us sat at opposite ends of the oval Regency table; Martin's chair would be against the wall between us, so he could join in the conversation, as well as serve us, but all I ever saw him consume was a mug of milky coffee. The first course was usually cold smoked salmon, asparagus, or a cold soup, followed by duck. Martin would grin wickedly and say, "Marks and Spencer."

Once he asked me where I thought the lunch had come from, so I naturally said, "Marks and Spencer?" He snorted dismissively, "Fortnum and Mason!" To this day I'm not sure if he was joking about where he shopped for those meals. What I do know is that my customary Christmas gift from Sir John of a bottle of champagne and box of champagne truffles came direct from Fortnum's.

The lunch table was set exquisitely with cut-glass goblets, fine porcelain, old silver, damask napkins, and a candelabra in the middle. We always ended with cheese and biscuits, though more of the latter were eaten by the three Tibetan terriers Arthur, Aaron and Simon as they waited patiently for Sir John to slip them their regular treat.

The housekeeper cooked the meal, and Martin served us. Domestic skills were not in the great actor's repertoire. Once I could only go down for the afternoon, and as I arrived Martin was going off to do the food-shopping for the week. He said, "Now, Gielgud, everything is prepared for tea, all you have to do is boil the kettle." At about half-past three Sir John said, "I'd better go and make the tea." After he was gone for nearly ten minutes I ventured out to the kitchen, where he said crossly, "This kettle refuses to boil!" When I looked at it, he had switched it on at the wall-plug, but not lifted the switch on the kettle itself. Clearly, he had never undertaken this simple task before.

His main meal for guests was luncheon, as he did not like late dinner-parties, but my wife and I did go down for an early dinner on a couple of occasions, when the cuisine was very similar to the lunches. He was the most charming host, and just in case his theatre stories might be boring Aileen, his conversation would move easily to reminiscences of dining with the Duke and Duchess of Windsor, or being mobbed with Richard Burton and Liz Taylor.

Many distinguished figures arrived at Wotton Underwood during the Gielgud tenure at South Pavilion. Some of these were friends from stage or screen—Anthony Hopkins, Irene Worth, Marti Stephens, Keith Baxter. Others came from rather different circles. When I was writing the biography of his great friend and stage-partner Ralph Richardson, the author Angela Huth told me of accompanying the Queen Mother to tea there, and being met in the garden by Sir John and Sir Ralph!

As we walked up to the house we paused as John showed the Queen Mother a couple of tortoises. She said, "I wonder how tortoises communicate with each other, do you think they speak to each other?" Ralph said, "Oh, Ma'am, would you like me to try and find out?" and he leaned over the wire and made as if to listen to the conversation of the tortoises, it was a very charming scene.

Then we went into the dining-room for tea, which looked like a banquet for a hundred people, and there were only six or seven of us; profiteroles done up in pyramids, with strawberries and sugar all interlaced falling down, fifteen different kinds of sandwiches, cakes and biscuits. Mr Richardson was at the end pouring tea, and I had the good fortune to be sitting opposite the Queen Mother, who had Ralph on one side and John on the other. They were competing with anecdotes to entertain her, and she was dazzlingly happy, turning from one to the other of the old knights. I thought I can't really believe this, it's just the most memorable tea of my life, nothing whatever will ever, ever surpass it."

I know what Angela felt, I never left Wotton without feeling that I was walking on air, not just from the Gielgud hospitality, but from the scintillating conversation, in which he never seemed to repeat himself. I remember those visits as unforgettable times with a great actor, a wonderful friend, and a perfect host.

An Actor's Life

A Song from The Bohemians

If I might choose my destiny
An Actor's lot be mine!
For half a dozen other lives
With his own life combine.

Tho' he's poor by fortune's malice,
And tho' his coat be bare and old,
Night bestows a regal palace,
And he'll robe, in cloth of gold!

Such is the player's magic story,
Passing quick from grave to gay,
Up and down,
Rags and crown,
Rich tomorrow poor today.

If larder lack, or cellar fail
What actor shoud repine?
He quaffs an empty cup
And on a wooden joint can dine!

Actors too can flourish after
The dagger sharp, the poison bowl!
Groaning's kill'd by sudden laughter
While a jolly song they'll troll!

Such is the player's magic story,
Passing quick from grave to gay,
Up and down,
Rags and crown,
In the self-same day!

H B Farnie (c1870)

35

CHAPTER EIGHT

Sir John Betjeman

1906-1984

John Betjeman was appointed poet laureate on the death of Cecil Day Lewis in 1972. "Lucky old England to have him," wrote his friend and fellow-poet Philip Larkin. Betjeman was already the best known and most loved poet of his generation. His witty, comic verse had a very wide appeal, reaching far beyond traditional poetry readers. Winner of the Queen's Gold Medal for poetry in 1960 and knighted in 1969, he was the poet of cosy suburbs and garden gnomes, of railways and churches, of England's countryside and provincial towns.

Betjeman was born in Highgate, north London. He was an only child and often felt lonely and insecure, feelings intensified by his father's deafness and his mother's unthinking chatter. He took comfort in his teddy bear, Archibald, who remained with him all his life. He was taught briefly at Highgate School by T S Eliot before going on to Marlborough, which he disliked, and then to Oxford where he made many friends and acquaintances, among them W H Auden and Louis MacNeice. A *bon viveur* and aesthete, he left the university without a degree. Determined not to enter the family business, at first he made his living from school-mastering and journalism. His first book of poems was published in 1931; his *Collected Poems*, which appeared in 1958, was particularly well received, as was *Summoned by Bells*, a long autobiographical poem which looked back to Wordsworth's Prelude.

Betjeman was happy to accept the laureateship, pleased to follow in the footsteps of Tennyson, one of his heroes. He asked that the traditional payment in drink, by now in abeyance, should be reinstated and he enjoyed sharing with his friends the wine and champagne sent by the Queen's wine merchant. But he found it difficult to write poems for particular occasions—Princess Anne's wedding in 1973, the Queen's Silver Jubilee in 1976. He worried that he would let his public down. In the last six years of his life, in increasingly poor health, he wrote very little. Yet at his death in 1984 his reputation remained high—popular poet, broadcaster, social historian, railway enthusiast, conservationist, humorist, very loveable Englishman.

How to Get on in Society

Published in 1954—an irresistible mix of affection and satire.

Phone for the fish-knives, Norman
As Cook is a little unnerved;
You kiddies have crumpled the serviettes
And I must have things daintily served.

Are the requisites all in the toilet?
The frills round the cutlets can wait
Till the girl has replenished the cruets
And switched on the logs in the grate.

It's ever so close in the lounge, dear,
But the vestibule's comfy for tea
And Howard is out riding on horseback
So do come and take some with me.

Now here is a fork for your pastries
And do use the couch for your feet;
I know what I wanted to ask you—
Is trifle sufficient for sweet?

Milk and then just as it comes dear?
I'm afraid the preserve's full of stones;
Beg pardon, I'm soiling the doileys
With afternoon tea-cakes and scones.

(from Verses of the Poets Laureate—*see Betjeman)*

Rules was one of the favourite restaurants of both Noel Coward and Graham Greene; however, Noel had to put up with reviews by Greene which were little more than personal attacks on him. He responded by sending Greene the following verses:

Oh there's many a heart beats faster lads
And swords from their sheathes flash keen
When round the embers——
——the glowing embers
Men crouch at Hallowe'en
And suddenly somebody remembers
The name of Graham Greene.
(A literary disaster lads
The fall of Graham Greene.)

Oh there's many a Catholic Priest my boys
And many a Rural Dean
Who, ages later——
——long ages later
When all has been, has been,
Will secretly read an old *Spectator*
And pray for Graham Greene.
(Let's hope its sales have decreased my boys
Because of Graham Greene.)

Oh there's many a bitter smile my boys
And many a sneer obscene
When any critic——
——a first-rate critic,
Becomes a "Might have been"
Through being as harsh and Jesuitic
As Mr Graham Greene.
(Restrain that cynical smile my boys,
To jeer is never worthwhile my boys.
Remember the rising bile my boys
Of Mr Graham Greene.)

CHAPTER NINE

John Galsworthy 1867-1933

Galsworthy was another patron of Rules. He dined there many times. He was awarded the Nobel Prize for Literature in 1932, and is best remembered for his novel *The Forsyte Saga,* which was later made into a highly successful television series. His plays *The Silver Box,* 1906, *Strife,* 1909 (which was successfully revived at the National Theatre in 1978) and *Justice* were about social reform and had a significant impact on the campaign for prison reform. His life was a fascinating one, and his novels are still read today.

Born into a well-to-do London family, John Galsworthy was the eldest of four children with two sisters and one brother. His parents had wanted him to become a lawyer like his father, and sent him on a round-the-world trip after he had left school in an effort to get his restlessness out of his system, but the attempt backfired; Galsworthy met Joseph Conrad on a sailing ship going from Australia to South Africa. Conrad was first mate on the ship, but already working on his first novel *Almayer's Folly.* The two men became friends and remained friends until Conrad's death in 1924. Galsworthy returned from this voyage determined to become a writer.

The subject of his first novel derived from his own experience. He had fallen in love with a woman who was at the time unhappily married to his cousin, Arthur Galsworthy. Ada, Arthur's wife, had had an unhappy life, being an illegitimate child who had been adopted by an elderly obstetrician who had died, leaving her fairly well off.

When John was twenty-eight, he and Ada, who was three years older, began an affair which they kept secret primarily out of consideration for John's father and because of the moral standards of the time. However after John's father's death in 1904 they lived openly together. Her husband then divorced her, and in the following year she and John were married.

Both during the ten years of their liaison and during their subsequent marriage, Ada encouraged him in his ambition to become a writer, acted as his secretary, and may have suggested to him that he use their love-affair as the foundation of his first novel *Jocelyn.* This novel is the story of a passionate love affair that ends happily in the marriage of the principal characters. Galsworthy later did not deny the origin of this novel, but was not proud of it in later years, not so much for what it said about him as on account of the lack of control of the writing and of the characters, in striking contrast to both features of his subsequent books.

The most well-known of these is *The Forsyte Saga* first published in 1931. Extending over three volumes it is not so much the story of a family as of a class that is idealised to the point of incredibility. There are a few well-bred ruffians, but very, very few. Almost all the men are officers and gentlemen, and what gentlemen! They never tell a lie, even if their lives were to depend on telling one, they are totally loyal, patriotic and are either of independent means or have worthwhile careers in the army or navy or in the colonial service. Needless to say, their manners are as impeccable as their clothes. The action, a term loosely used, takes place against a background of London clubs, country houses, devoted servants and tenants, and only towards the end of the novel after the great depression has hit England is there any talk of people having to work for a living, being short of money or other mundane subjects.

The incidents revolve mostly around romantic relationships of a proper, conventional sort; misunderstandings abound and are usually cleared up through the intervention of benevolent, well-intentioned, incredibly noble members of the aristocracy or the church.

The ladies are marginally more interesting, a shade less perfect. They tell white lies to avoid embarrassment, can even consider the possibility of going to bed with a lover before they are married to him, though of course they never do, and aid and abet one another in the pursuit of love.

Both men and women are literate and indeed cultivated; there are frequent references in their conversation and thoughts to the Italian Renaissance, and except for the affectation on the part of one or two of dropping the final letter in "ing"s, no hint of anything less than perfect grammar rears its ugly head.

It is difficult nowadays to understand the popularity of Galsworthy's books in the 'thirties and 'forties except as romantic escapist fiction to distract people from the miseries of the Depression and the anxieties of the war years.

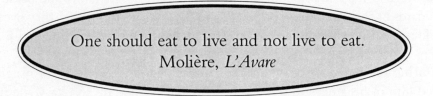
One should eat to live and not live to eat.
Molière, *L'Avare*

CHAPTER TEN

Rupert Brooke

Rupert Brooke was part of a generation of poets who were all but wiped out between 1914 and 1918. Brooke died in 1915 on his way to fight at Gallipoli. D H Lawrence, John Masefield, Walter de la Mare and Siegfried Sassoon all praised the poet whom Yeats had considered the handsomest man in England. His poem became almost a requiem for the men who lost their lives in the Great War.

> "If I should die, think only this of me
> That there's some corner of a foreign field
> That is forever England."

Here is an extract from one of his finest poems, "The Dining Room Tea".

> "When you were there, and you, and you,
> Happiness crowned the night; I too,
> Laughing and looking, one of all,
> I watched the quivering lamplight fall
> On plate and flowers and pouring tea
> And cup and cloth, and they and we
> Flung all the dancing moments by
> With jest and glitter. Lip and eye
> Flashed on the glory, shone and cried,
> Improvident, unmemoried;
> And fitfully and like a flame
> The light of laughter went and came.
> Proud in their careless transience moved
> The changing faces that I loved.

I saw the marble cup; the tea,
Hung on the air, an amber stream;
I saw the fire's unglittering gleam,
The painted flame, the frozen smoke.
The peace that lay, the light that shone.
You never knew that I had gone
A million miles away, and stayed
A million years. The laughter played
Unbroken round me; and the jest
Flashed on. And we that knew the best
Down wonderful hours grew happier yet.
I sang at heart, and talked, and ate,
And lived from laugh to laugh, I too,
When you were there, and you, and you."

Ruth Montagu, a friend, who was present at the tea, recalled:

"…in return for tea my Mother and I were invited to spend the day at the camp at Clifford Bridge she rode her bicycle and I my pony returning in the dark. As I was young, Rupert and Justin decided that a ball game was the best way to entertain me. I remember an enormous meal of stew cooked by my brother Paul, in which someone discovered a button. Afterwards we watched Rupert looking very beautiful swimming up and down in the river."

Brooke was often homesick for England when he was in the States and Canada. He wrote:

"Would God were eating plover's eggs
And drinking dry champagne
With the Bernard Shaws, Mr & Mrs Masefield,
Lady Horner, Neil Primrose, Raleigh, The Right
Honourable Augustine Birrell, Eddie, six or
Seven Asquiths, & Felicity Tree, in Downing Street again."

In 1915 Brooke died on the Greek island of Skyros, and is buried there.

CHAPTER ELEVEN

Somerset Maugham

Cakes and Ale

Dost thou think, because thou art virtuous, there shall be no more cakes and ale?

Probably none of Maugham's characters is as sympathetic to the contemporary reader as is Rosie, the protagonist of *Cakes and Ale*. It is highly possible that to some extent the novel is autobiographical. Ashenden, the persona that Maugham adopted in several of his books, and who appears in this novel as a twenty-one-year-old medical student, is the narrator, and irritates, as Maugham probably did in real life, by his fusty outmoded snobbery and his intellectual condescension.

Given the interest that Maugham clearly had in prostitutes, who appear as likeable characters in *Of Human Bondage* and in many of his short stories, it is not inconceivable that he had more than a literary interest in them when he was a medical student. It is also true that Maugham had more than a passing interest in food, was a somewhat fastidious gourmet, and gastronomy plays a central role in at least one of his short stories, "The Fat Ladies of Antibes", and in *Cakes and Ale*, where Rosie is wined and dined by many of her suitors in celebrated London restaurants such as Romano's.

Rosie likes pleasure of all kinds, sees no other purpose in life, and although she had been a barmaid, not a prostitute, has no attachment to or regard for the conventional sexual morality of her time. The title of the book does indicate her dislike of any puritan disdain of pleasure and of simple enjoyment, whether of food, clothes, money or sex. Rosie is portrayed as an affectionate good-time-girl, not impressed by honesty in money matters, and as willing to share her physical charms as her own and other people's money.

Much is made by Angus Wilson of Maugham's catty and malicious picture in this novel of the literary life of his time, with its account of the social climbing of authors, the patronage of them by rich ladies and their jealousies and scheming, no doubt caricatures recognisable by well-informed contemporaries, but this is of little interest now. What survives are his characters, mostly cynically drawn, except in the case of Rosie and her first husband, a struggling writer who ends up as a grand old man of English literature, saddened by his ill-advised decision to let Rosie go for the sake of his reputation, though he had been complaisant enough about her numerous affairs in his youth.

Although playwrights, we hope, do not have to submit themselves to social and other climbing in these days, nonetheless a rich member of the aristocracy as patron can probably be of great help to a struggling dramatist still. Noel Coward knew this as well when he became friends with the Duke of Kent.

The love of Rosie's life is a poorly educated and dishonest builder, flashily dressed and clearly (to the reader, though not to Rosie) someone who is not a gentleman. She had an affair with him before her first marriage, and when he had to escape his indebtedness by bolting to London, went with him. He is very much her male counterpart, and when he goes to America to make a fresh start, she goes with him and marries him. Perhaps to her surprise he is successful in America, and at the end of the book has left her a rich widow living in Yonkers, which she likes because it reminds her of England.

Maugham himself was no puritan, and had little time for his upright brother, who became Lord Chancellor of England. He probably felt, as did his contemporary Richard Findlater, that English drama had been in decline since Shakespeare, largely due to the Puritan influence which abolished theatre in the first place, and after its revival continued to have a depressing effect on its development, especially when puritanism re-surfaced in the Victorian era. The cult of restraint in acting and playwriting was, however, hardly distasteful to him, being himself so subject to it in life as well as in writing.

Findlater, in his book, *The Unholy Trade*, writes:

In this age of monstrous shadows and mechanical giants, the glory of the theatre and the guarantee of its immortality is the variable, undependable, inefficient human being who is the instrument and object of theatrical art. It is through the living actor, miraculously fallible, that the poet can meet the people and himself. The Chinese wall between highbrow and lowbrow may be melted down, and the prisoners liberated from their ivory towers. It is in the playhouse and only in the playhouse, that men may share the kindling experience of creation, in communion with each other, with the dead and with the mummers on the stage, and they may live, for a while, with the intensity, beauty and meaning that no celluloid reel can provide. That is why the theatre is indestructible. Its resources are inexhaustible, because they are the resources of naked human genius. Its power is immortal, because it is made not by machines but by men. Its range is infinite, because it is the range of the human spirit."

CHAPTER TWELVE

Terence Rattigan (1911–1977)

He was one of the most successful playwrights of his era. He celebrated his successful opening nights, as did Noel Coward, at the Ivy and the Caprice. Both playwrights were attacked by the critic Kenneth Tynan. Yet Rattigan was knighted in 1976. His play, *French without Tears*, ran for a thousand performances, as did *While the Sun Shines*. His other plays include *Love in Idleness, Who is Sylvia?, The Sleeping Prince, Flare Path, The Browning Version, The Deep Blue Sea* and original film scripts *The Way to the Stars, The VIPs* with Richard Burton and Elizabeth Taylor, and *The Yellow Rolls-Royce* with Rex Harrison.

Many of the British plays were thought to be "whimsical". Terence Rattigan volunteered to write an article for the *New York Times* himself, to defend the English theatre from the charge that it was "escapist so it is dead". Accepting that O'Neill and other American playwrights wrote plays that face the modern world and its problems fearlessly, showing life as it is in all its harassing aspects and providing some message for its betterment, he insisted that the English theatre was by no means dead, even if its audience preferred escapism. "From Shakespeare until Shaw Englishmen continued to go to the theatre to escape from the immediate problems of everyday life. They went to Galsworthy's plays because he was a superb technician and gave them characters that were real and situations which they found exciting. I don't honestly believe they cared much for the message which either of these dramatists contributed."

In a very thinly veiled defence of his own play, Rattigan concluded:

"Whimsy is a word on every American critic's tongue in writing of English plays. (I can say this without prejudice. The word was not mentioned once in reviews of French Without Tears to my grateful surprise.) It is used exclusively as a term of opprobrium and applies to almost any play that is not firmly rooted in mother earth. One might be permitted to wonder what kind of reviews A Midsummer Night's Dream would receive from the New York critics in their present mood if they were seeing the play for the first time."

It was evidence of his sensitivity to criticism. And his first experience in New York set the tone for years to come. No matter how much he tried to make light of criticism, it hurt him deeply. (His first four plays on Broadway were flops, the first success was when Alfred Lunt and Lynn Fontanne took the leads in *Oh Mistress Mine*. Just to continue on this subject for a while, the whole concept of play scripts has radically changed over the past fifty years, as all theatre-goers know, and today we have nudity, swearing, drug-taking on stage as well as the reality of what is happening in the world, politically and socially. Some argue that this is for the better, but the older generation remember the evenings when play-going was not an insult to one's sensibilities, or embarrassing, and the experience was therefore perhaps more pleasant but just as challenging. George Bernard Shaw's and Harley Granville Barker's plays were and still are illustrations of this. Intelligent ideas were discussed, class barriers exposed, brilliant plots conceived, and actors found rewarding roles to play. American playwrights were writing about different subjects, so when the British plays were first brought to New York, they sometime seemed out of place with their society manners and drawing-room comedies.

The biographer of Terence Rattigan, Geoffrey Wansell, writes that he was a child of the Osborne generation, weaned at the Royal Court, on the *Observer* reviews of Kenneth Tynan and on a diet of Arnold Wesker, Joan Littlewood and Harold Pinter. Most of the older generation loathed the new "Angry young men". Geoffrey was convinced that the world of drawing-rooms and French windows, of elegant dresses and gentlemen in dinner-jackets was doomed, and says he argued with his father who was convinced that the "kitchen sink" would eventually disappear down its own plug-hole; and that, in any case, it did not hold a candle to Rattigan. Though his work never lost its appeal to the ordinary theatre-goer, it did so to those who commanded the heights of the British theatre in the years after 1956. So Wansell says, as he researches his work.

> Edmund Kean, the great flamboyant nineteenth century actor, is said to have varied his diet according to the part he had to play. For tyrants he would eat roast pork. For murderers, raw beef. For lovers, boiled mutton. There is no record of the roles he played when he ate ham.

Lilian Baylis, c 1933. Other guests include Charles Laughton, Flora Robson, Athene Seyer, James Mason, Elsa Lanchester, Tyrone Guthrie, Alan Napier.

1st May 1956, celebration at Binkie Beaumont's home at 14 Lord North Street in honour of Dame Sybil ...ning the Phoenix Theatre Company, with Paul Scofield, Sybil Thorndike, Lewis Casson and Peter Brook.

3 Above: At the Ivy: Vi[vien] Leigh, Kay Kendall, Laure[n] Bacall with Noel Coward.

4 Left: John Miller with John Gielgud.

5 *Above: Author with Kenneth Branagh at Criterion Gala for Sir John Gielgud after the showing of his film,* Swan Song. *(The film as an adaptation of the Chekhov play, in which Sir John starred.)*

Right: Simpsons-in-the-Strand, interior.

7 *Top Far left: Criterion Restaurant.*

8 *Bottom far left: The Salisbury, St Martin's Lane.*

9 *Left: Simpsons-in-the-Strand, entrance.*

10 *Below: the Ivy.*

11 Above: Sheekey's in St Martin's Court.

12 Below: Julian Slade with Michael Law. Slade, the composer of Salad Days, meets Law whose orchestra, Piccadilly Dance Orchestra, plays at the Savoy Hotel. Law is a singer/pianist and conductor of the band.

13 Above right: The author with Lord Richard Attenborough at the Ivy.

14 Above far right: The Grill Room at the Café Royal.

15 Below far right: Alexander H Cohen with Sir John Gielgud and Vivien Leigh.

16 Right: Kaspar the cat at the Savoy. A tradition of the Savoy has it that, if the number of diners amounts to an unlucky thirteen, Kaspar the cat is placed on the fourteenth seat, complete with napkin around his neck, to restore good fortune.

17 Below left: An original cocktail shaker which was used in the American bar in the 1930s.

18 Below right: Vivien Leigh, a painting by Gary George.

CHAPTER THIRTEEN

Gala Celebration

Sybil Thorndike and Lewis Casson were the most popular and successful theatrical couple in London for many years, the predecessors of the Oliviers. After touring America with Ben Great, Sybil had a long career on the London stage. Originally she wanted to become a concert pianist and studied at the Guildhall School of Music. However she found she had a weak wrist that gave her great pain, so she discontinued her music career. Her acting career included playing at the Old Vic, and later she originated the role of St Joan in George Bernard Shaw's play. They were Mr and Mrs Theatre in London for over twenty years. She was appointed DBE in 1931 and Companion of Honour in 1966, and at her final performance in 1966 she inaugurated a new theatre in Surrey, named after her.

Lewis Casson 1875–1969

Knighted in 1945, he became the leading force in CEMA (Council for the Encouragement of Music and the Arts) directing and playing in *Macbeth* for the first tour of the Welsh coalmines in 1940.

After the war he continued to mix acting (in plays ranging from Shaw to Shakespeare to Euripides) with directing, and, with his wife Sybil, frequently toured abroad in both plays and recitals.

Sir Alec Guinness recounts in his book *Blessings in Disguise* how kind they were to him when he first met them. He saw them when he was a schoolboy and wrote a letter to Sybil asking how they made the rain and thunder in the play he had seen them in. She wrote back inviting him backstage and Lewis showed him the thunder machine, a great iron sheet suspended from the flies. The two of them worked hard at rain-making for a few minutes. "I was merciless and never asked them to stop." Finally they straightened up and Lewis, quite puffed, said abruptly, "That's all we can show you." Here is what their son John Casson wrote:

On Sunday 22nd December, 1968, we gave a party to celebrate their Diamond Wedding. It was quite a big party as our parties go, for there were something like ninety people in the Holland Park flat that we had been lent by some very dear friends.

"Don't let's do anything elaborate," Patricia had said. "We'll give them champagne to drink, and mince pies to eat because it's Christmas." And so she made two or three hundred mince pies and I ordered four dozen bottles of champagne, which by all the caterers' guidebooks should have been more than enough for ninety people. In the event, we had two bottles left after the party and not a single mince pie. But there were a lot of happy people, happy to be there, proud to know each other and all thrilled to have the chance of giving their love and affection to Sybil and Lewis.

Oh, the memories that came crowding in! I remembered meeting Emlyn Williams for the first time at the end of August, 1939, when he and Sybil were both playing in *The Corn is Green* at the Piccadilly. I went to see Sybil in her dressing-room before catching the night train at Euston to join the cruiser *Southampton* at Scapa Flow. We saw a lot of him again in 1955 when he was captivating Australian audiences with his readings of Dickens and Dylan Thomas. One night after his show he and Robert Helpmann came for supper to our house in Melbourne. The party went on till five the next morning while each of them capped the stories of the other. After he and his wife had greeted Sybil and Lewis for their diamond wedding he looked round at the gathering and said, "My God, if a bomb fell on this lot there'd be no London theatre left!"

Patricia had briefed my niece Diana and her American husband Bill Graham, to collect people's hats and coats as they came in. They were on a sort of extended honeymoon from their job of teaching drama at the University of Minnesota. They were both, therefore, theatre-minded. Bill, however, hadn't ever met many of the top actors. He never really recovered from the moment when he opened the door of our flat to be confronted by his hero John Gielgud dressed in a hat and coat of black sable. He took the garments like a somnambulist and was seen carrying them off to the cloakroom rather like a neophyte taking part in some esoteric ceremony. Dear John Gielgud, who had been Prospero in *The Tempest* with Lewis as Gonzalo on the night in 1940 when Sybil came to the theatre with the news that I had not returned from a raid over Norway. He too had come to our home in Australia and we had one of those lovely long rambling lunches that you hope are never going to end. We had all told stories of Sybil and Lewis and they were warm friendly and witty stories so that the afternoon had a sort of glow to it that came from the words rather than the wine.

The guests continued to pour in. The Liveseys, Roger and Ursula, who are almost part of every part of the family, the Redgraves, the Attenboroughs, Tarquin Olivier, Sybil's godson, with his wife and his mother, Jill Esmond (who had sent me lovely parcels from U.S.A. when I was a prisoner in Germany). Larry Olivier, to his and our sorrow, wasn't well that day and couldn't be there. We had played together in Carlyle Square and at his father's vicarage when we were children and we had all been firmly and gently taken charge of by his elder sister Sybille. Larry is a couple of years my senior and when he joined the Fleet Air Arm at the beginning of the war I had rather hoped that I might perhaps find myself as his squadron commander. But it was not to be and I had to content myself with being called "Sir" by Lieutenant Ralph Richardson when, as a strange Lieutenant-Commander, I offered him a gin one night in the mess at an R.N. Air Station near Southampton.

The list of guests goes on and on and the endless stream of memories is deluging my mind. There were so many more, each with vivid pictures surrounding them. Joyce and Reggie Grenfell, whom we always seem to be meeting in different parts of the world. Peggy Ashcroft whom I first remember with Sybil in the memorable Paul Robeson *Othello*, at the Savoy. Margaret Rutherford and Stringer Davis, Carlton Hobbs (Hobbo) and his wife. The Michael MacOwans and, bless her, the oldest lady of the theatre, Ellaline Terris, at 98 well aware that she was the grande-dame over them all moving through the room like an empress.

When I was sixteen there was a charity matinee of *Quality Street* played by the children of actors and actresses. I was lucky enough to be playing Valentine Brown and after it was over Ellaline Terris and her husband, Sir Seymour Hicks, came to see us. "My boy," said Sir Seymour, "I played this part twenty years ago." And then he told me at some length how he played it, and then said, "But you were splendid, my boy, splendid." I wish I had seen him play it. Who has ever played comedy with his style and flourish? Two days later I received a parcel with a book inside it. It was called *Difficulties* and was written and indeed signed by Sir Seymour. It was about the problems that a young man faces in coping with the "facts of life". I have often wondered whether the book was meant to help me as an actor or as a sailor. He had seen me attempting to be the former and had been told that my calling was the latter.

We finished the last of the champagne and the marvellous party was over. "Aren't they marvellous?" went on echoing in my mind. I must think about it, think back of my years with them. They certainly have been marvellous and we have all had a lot of fun together in one way and another and a few fights too in a not very unfriendly way. What is the magic? What's the secret? What have the two of them got in greater abundance than the rest of us? As a first approximation I should think it is a passionate enthusiasm for living and an almost total dedication to exploring and practising the art of living in terms of acting. Marvellous! I must think about it.

Heaven sends us good meat, but the Devil sends cooks.
David Garrick

That all softening, overpowering knell
The tocsin of the soul—the dinner bell.
Lord Byron

This piece of cod passes all understanding
Sir Edward Lutyens

Fame is at best an unperforming cheat;
But 'tis substantial happiness to eat.
Alexander Pope

There is no love sincerer than the love of food.
George Bernard Shaw

Oscar Wilde said…

It is only shallow people who do not judge by appearances.

It is better to be beautiful than to be good. But…it is better to be good than to be ugly.

There is no such thing as a moral or an immoral book. Books are well written, or badly written.

CHAPTER FOURTEEN

Sir Alec Guinness

Bridge over the River Kwai, The Lavender Hill Mob, Kind Hearts and Coronets were some of the most famous films of Alec Guinness. But like many other British actors he did not become famous until after he started making movies, even though he had been a well-known stage actor, beginning his career at the Old Vic. He was fired by Lilian Baylis when he was very young, and he was devastated when she told him that he couldn't act.

Ernest Milton, another brilliant actor whom Guinness described as a unique talent touched with genius, worked in London successfully for over forty years although he was originally from San Francisco. He too started his career, after arriving in London, at the Old Vic, and he told Guinness that the only woman who really aroused him physically was Lilian Baylis, the founder of the Old Vic, a dour, bespectacled heavy-set woman who had a slight squint and wore an academic gown over her tweeds and woollies.

Alec invited Ernest to lunch one day at a new restaurant in Covent Garden, where unfortunately they were served a "revolting, pretentious dinner". Ernest worked himself up into a frenzy when talking about another actor's interpretation of Hamlet, which he had seen forty years previously. "He stole all his best readings from me," he said, thumping the table. "You remember the way I said, 'The potent poison quite o'er-crows my spirit'?" He rose from the table and gave the line a full Drury Lane treatment, bawling out, "the potent POISON", to the consternation of the other diners, who dropped their forks with horror, wondering if they were eating the same dish. There were furtive looks towards his plate. "I had to hurry him away past the scowls of the pompous waiters, never to darken their doors again. Not long afterwards the restaurant closed its doors for good. Perhaps Ernest had put a curse on it. I certainly did; but Ernest's would have been more potent."

The other story involves Dame Edith Evans, whom he invited to lunch at the Mirabelle.

"She was in good form but rather anxious, on my behalf, at what the bill might come to. 'Not to worry,' I said, 'I'm filming.' Rather coyly, after a lot of looking at me sideways, she was bold enough to ask what I was being paid. It was *The Lavender Hill Mob* I was making and I told her I was getting £6,000 for the job.

I might have stabbed her with a fish-fork. She fell back in her chair, agony written all over her face. 'Six thousand pounds?' I repeated it, thinking to myself, 'Oh Lord, perhaps I undersold myself; should have held out for ten.' But it was the vast size of the amount which had dumbfounded her. She became very grave. 'I must make another film,' she said. 'Or do you call them movies?'

" 'The money is the same, whatever you may call them.'

" 'And you enjoy it?'

" 'Quite,' I said, truthfully. A certain impatience was detectable in the rest of her meal; she got through her Bombe Surprise in a flash, anxious, I believe, to get to a telephone to call her agent."

Another close friend was Sir Ralph Richardson, and they often worked together. He tells of a dinner at the Connaught when Ralph only wanted a Spanish omelette.

"He always has a Spanish omelette,' explained his wife. Finally Ralph said, 'Would you forgive me, old fellow, if I went home now?'

" 'Of course,' I said. 'Are you unwell?'

" 'No. Bored. I'd rather go home.'

"He rose from the table and I followed him. He caught his foot in a chair and fell flat on his face. I went to help him but he managed to pull me down on top of him. I offered to get him a taxi but he said he would prefer to walk. I watched him amble away across Carlos Place, day-dreaming and looking forlorn. He must have day-dreamed a lot as a boy, and continued to do so through a long life, for I often thought that the things he said were not always invented on the spur of the moment but were dredged up from years of contemplation. A day or two after our non-dinner at the Connaught he telephoned me.

" 'Did you walk all the way home?' I asked.

" 'Yes,' he replied. 'But I sat for a while on a bench in Oxford Street. It was very nice until a chap on a bicycle stopped by me. 'I know you,' he said. 'Oh, yes?' I said. 'Yes,' he said. 'You're Sir John Gielgud,' he said. 'Fuck off!' I said. Then I walked home. It was a lovely night for walking. So many stars.'"

Finally Alec tells us about his luncheon with George Bernard Shaw. Shaw invited him and his wife with a niece of Mrs. Shaw's and Sir Sydney Carlyle Cockerall, formerly curator of the Fitzwilliam Museum in Cambridge.

Mrs. Shaw received them in their London home at Whitehall Court, and showed them their picture collection which Guinness found hideous.

"She kept up a general chicken-like clucking which meant we hardly had to utter a word. As the clock struck one, a big mahogany door was thrown open by a servant in braided uniform and white gloves who announced, as if at an embassy reception 'Mr. Shaw'. Guinness went to shake his hand, but because of Shaw's bad eyesight missed him by a yard. They went out of the drawing room into the rather dingy dining room and two more servants pulled out their chairs to be seated. Alec's wife, knowing Shaw was a vegetarian, had predicted that they would be served nut cutlets and dewberry soup, but they were surprised to be served roast chicken and white wine, while the Shaws pushed little bits of greenery around their plates and sipped water. However, what Guinness noticed was Shaw's almost eighteenth-century courtesy.

"Shaw's manners were a delightful mixture of formality, ease and charm, of a sort rarely encountered nowadays, except in the very old and very distinguished. Sir Osbert Sitwell had the same cultivated gift, as did the U.S. Ambassador to Britain, Mr Douglas, the film director Anthony Asquith and, still in our midst, Lord Stockton and King Hussein of Jordan men who manage to make civilisation appear attainable."

Ham Actor

Athene Seyler was a wonderful actress who lived to be over 100. She went to lunch at the Ritz in her younger days. She chose between one of two rather stylish hats. When she got to the restaurant she noticed at the next door table a woman wearing the identical hat. So she got her attention, pointed at her own hat, pointed at the other woman's and made a funny face, expressing horror at the coincidence. The other woman looked rather confused and mystified and a bit hurt. Only when Athene Seyler got home did she notice that she had chosen the other hat, so was not wearing the same hat as the other woman at all.

CHAPTER FIFTEEN

Sydney Smith 1771–1845

Twelve Miles from a Lemon

This is the title of a new book of Sydney Smith's selected writings and sayings. Born in 1771, he was the Canon of St Paul's, and a selection from his writings appeared in 1885, then his *Wit and Wisdom* in 1861. He was a clergyman, magistrate and village doctor in Somerset, and then given a resident canonry at St Paul's. A lover of justice and truth, he was a life-long defender of the oppressed. His failure to rise higher in the Church is attributed to his wide reputation as a master of wit and satire. He is ranked among the premier English wits, and has been compared to Swift and to Voltaire.

Recipe for a Salad

> To make this condiment, your poet begs
> The pounded yellow of two hard-boiled eggs;
> Two boiled potatoes, passed through kitchen-sieve,
> Smoothness and softness to the salad give;
> Let onion atoms lurk within the bowl,
> And, half-suspected, animate the whole.
> Of mordant mustard add a single spoon,
> Distrust the condiment that bites so soon;
> But deem it not, thou man of herbs, a fault,
> To add a double quantity of salt.
> And, lastly, o'er the flavored compound toss
> A magic soup-spoon of anchovy sauce.
> Oh, green and glorious! Oh, herbaceous treat!
> 'T would tempt the dying anchorite to eat;

Back to the world he'd turn his fleeting soul,
And plunge his fingers in the salad bowl!
Serenely full, the epicure would say,
Fate can not harm me, I have dined to-day!

Sagittarius (Olga Katzin) 1896–1987

The Passionate Profiteer to his Love (After Christopher Marlowe)

Come feed with me and be my love,
And pleasures of the table prove,
Where Prunier and the Ivy yield
Choice dainties of the stream and field.

At Claridge's thou shalt duckling eat,
Sip vintages both dry and sweet,
And thou shalt squeeze between thy lips
Asparagus with buttered tips.
On caviare my love shall graze,
And plump on salmon mayonnaise,
And browse at Scott's beside thy swain
On lobster Newburg with champagne.

Come share at the Savoy with me
The menu of austerity;
If in these pastures thou wouldst rove
Then feed with me and be my love.

CHAPTER SIXTEEN

Vivien Leigh

Most Americans will remember Vivien Leigh as Scarlett O'Hara in *Gone with the Wind*, but most British people remember her for her stage roles particularly when partnered by Laurence Olivier. Her theatre career began long before her film career, and one of her most important theatrical challenges was when she was trying to prevent the demolition of the St James's Theatre without success. She said, "It's extraordinary. If I go into a restaurant, quite quietly, everybody turns and looks. Now I walk down the Strand, ringing a bell and nobody pays any attention at all!"

When Laurence Olivier bought as their home the Elizabethan country manor house called Notley Abbey at the height of his success, Vivien was very upset because the Abbey needed to be totally renovated and decorated, a daunting task which she knew she would have to do. She eventually loved the place and entertained constantly with a guest list of celebrities both from the theatre and films driving down every weekend. There are many reports on what an exquisite hostess she was, thinking of every request made by a house guest and providing lavish meals and picnics both indoors and outdoors in the summer.

One of Vivien's favourite restaurants in London was the Caprice in Arlington Street. She liked French vegetables, especially fennel; baby lamb was a favourite, and it was Lord Olivier's too.

The Oliviers looked a curious couple to Larry Adler, the composer and harmonica player who had co-starred with Vivien in St Martin's Lane, when he walked into the Caprice for lunch in the first week of July 1957. They sat together on a banquette just past the little podium where Mario, the maitre d'hotel, kept his "bible" of reservations. Vivien looked flushed and excited; Olivier, hunched and grim.

"Larry...Larry," she called out to Adler, "come and join my march."

Her tone was so penetrating and imperious that the gossip in the fashionable restaurant was hushed; the audience listened expectantly. "Larry," Vivien said agitatedly, "we're going to march on Parliament to save the St James's Theatre from being knocked down by that awful property developer. You must join us."

The 122-year-old theatre, the citadel of Olivier's actor-management endeavours, was going to be torn down to make way for an office block. Privately, Olivier acknowledged he could never make the St James's pay: it was sad, but there it was. Vivien had other views.

"I'm an American…I can't march on Parliament," Adler protested. Vivien raised her voice to sergeant-major level. "How dare you contradict me…You must join me."

Adler then recalls that Olivier gave him a look "which said to me, 'Larry, get the hell out of here,' which I did."

A few days later, on 10th July, escorted by a sheepish Alan Dent and not many others, Vivien led her "march" along the Strand swinging a hand-bell. Two days after that, she interrupted a House of Lords debate and was escorted from the precincts of Westminster by the gentlemen usher know as Black Rod. Even a £500 donation from Churchill and a letter from him admiring her courage, but disapproving, "as a Parliamentarian", of her disorderly method, did not win the day for Vivien or the St James's.

No mean woman can cook well, for it calls for a light hand, a generous spirit and a large heart.
Paul Gauguin

Every night should have its own menu.
Honoré de Balzac
There comes a time in every woman's life when the only thing that helps is a glass of champagne.
Bette Davis, *Old Acquaintance*

Larry ordered an enormous meal—a salad with blue cheese dressing, a huge steak, onion rings. This, it appeared, was what Vivien had always ordered—it was, I guessed, in honor of her memory that he had ordered all this, not for himself. It came back to me that, for all her slender figure, Vivien had had a hearty appetite—rather like Scarlett O'Hara. Many a time I had seen her put away a huge meal, huge even by my standards, and I was a teenage boy. When it came time for dessert Larry ordered what she had apparently always ordered here: three scoops of vanilla ice cream covered with green crème de menthe. He did not touch this, either—he was content to stare at it as it melted before him.
Michael Korda

CHAPTER SEVENTEEN

Afternoon Tea and Chocolates

Up to the 1950s in most theatres in London, before the performance of a play one could buy afternoon tea on a tray, which was passed along the row to your seat at intermission. On the tray would be a pot of tea or coffee, two digestive biscuits and a slice of fruit cake. Nowadays, patrons are often distracted by the ringing of cell phones usually at some dramatic moment in the play, yet in those days the dramatic moment was often shattered by the crashing of a cup or a tray uncollected by an usherette.

The trays were collected at the end of the intermission, just before the next act began, and sometimes patrons in the front row of the stalls would place their trays on the stage for the usherette to collect. Many times, especially at the Old Vic Theatre, which had an open-thrust stage, there would be a whole row of trays along the stage, which had to be rescued as the house lights went down.

Noel Coward described this problem in one of his short stories, "Ashes of Roses". The scene takes place in the dressing room of the lead actress and the producer, Mr. Gilmore. He says:

"Everything all right? No complaints?"

Leonora replies: "A million complaints." Leonora patted his mottled red face affectionately. "Those damned girls with their coffee trays rattling all through the beginning of the second act—one of these nights I shall jump over the orchestra pit and bash their heads in!"

"All right, all right." He held up his hand pacifically. "It won't happen tomorrow night, I promise."

"Does that go for tea as well? Tomorrow's a matinee day!"

"Tea trays out before the curtain—cross my heart," said Mr Gilmore. "Goodnight, my dear."

Another annoyance, sanctified by tradition, was the rustling of chocolate boxes and wrappers, the chocolates having been bought at the bar or brought to the theatre. This rustling could continue right through the performance, but happily this tradition is fast disappearing in most theatres today, especially in Britain.

It must be that play-going makes people hungry, because it is a well-known historical fact that the longer the play the bigger the boxes of chocolate dragged into the theatre.

Chocolates

Here the seats are: George, old man,
Get some chocolates while you can.

Quick, the curtain's going to rise,
(Either Bradbury's or Spry's).

"The Castle ramparts, Elsinore"
(That's not sufficient, get some more).

There's the Ghost; he does look wan
(Help yourself, and pass them on).

Doesn't Hamlet do it well?
(This one is a caramel).

Polonius's beard is fine
(Don't you grab: that big one's mine).

Look the King can't bear the play
(Throw that squashy one away).

Now the King is at his prayers
(Splendid, there are two more layers).

Hamlet's going for his mother
(Come on, Tony, have another).

Poor Ophelia! Look, she's mad
(However many's Betty had?)

The Queen is dead and so's the King
(Keep that lovely silver string).

Now even Hamlet can no more
(Pig! You've dropped it on the floor).

That last Act's simply full of shocks
(There's several left, so bring the box).

Guy Boas (1925)

59

CHAPTER EIGHTEEN

Sausages on Stage

Emma Cons was the woman who founded the Old Vic and her work was carried on by Lilian Baylis, one of the many deeply inspired individuals who were successful in their endeavours against so many obstacles in keeping the artistic spirit alive. We are so fortunate to have such legacies left by such pioneers. That's what makes the theatre scene so historic and exciting in London. Their monuments are still here—Henry Irving's Lyceum Theatre, Sheridan's Drury Lane, Lillian Baylis at the Old Vic and now of course the new Globe Theatre. People who visit London and miss all this, miss the central core of theatrical and artistic London.

If you think of all the unsigned contracts and choices offered to go elsewhere that are dished out to the leading actors and actresses, you would quickly realise how much they are focused on carrying on a tradition that is legendary. We lose a few to Hollywood, Richard Burton in the 'fifties and now Anthony Hopkins, but the others are not so easily seduced.

The Old Vic Theatre was originally built in 1818 and was named the Royal Coburg after one of the donors, Prince Leopold. Unfortunately the theatre was located in a bad area and it became the home of melodramas and crude music hall shows. By 1880 it had just closed and then Emma Cons, a social reformer bought it and redecorated it.

She began by forbidding alcohol, renaming it The Royal Victoria Coffee House, and starting a completely new policy of presenting concerts, musical evenings with extracts from opera, and temperance meetings. To make ends meet, she also opened a college in the rear of the theatre called Morley College. As the work increased, she asked her niece Lilian Baylis, who was a music teacher in South Africa to join her as her assistant.

When Emma Cons died in 1912, Lilian Baylis took over the theatre. She immediately applied for and obtained a licence to produce operas and plays, and two years later she had formed her own drama and opera company. Because there was so little space in the building for dressing rooms, rehearsal and backstage areas, she moved Morley College out in 1923 and had more of a free hand for opera and play productions. She was a religious woman, usually going to mass in the morning on her way to the theatre. It is said that she would often pray, "Please God, send me a good actor, but send him cheap." She would cook her meals on a gas ring, beside the stage, so quite often the smell of fried sausages drifted across the stage during rehearsals.

Ben Greet became her first resident director for drama and the opera company was run by Clive Barrey and Edward Dent who translated every opera into English. A financial crisis arose and Charles Dance, the impresario, donated £30,000—so that in the 1923-1924 season the Vic staged twenty operas and eighteen plays, most of them by Shakespeare.

In the 1920s, she helped purchase the old Sadler's Wells Theatre in Islington, where more opera could be heard at reasonable prices, and helped Ninette de Valois to start her ballet company which eventually became the Royal Ballet. Her energy and planning was astonishing. She hired directors, actors and set designers. Thus began her illustrious career, which helped so much to bring such talented performers as Sybil Thorndike, Edith Evans, Peggy Ashcroft, Michael Redgrave, Alec Guinness, Laurence Olivier, John Gielgud, not forgetting directors such as Tyrone Guthrie.

Lilian Baylis died in 1937, but not before laying down the idea for a National Theatre. The theatre continued until 1941—when it was bombed. The company decamped to the New Theatre until the Old Vic re-opened in 1950.

The new National Theatre was established in 1963 at the Old Vic under the direction of Laurence Olivier, and in 1976 the National moved to its present home on the South Bank. Lilian Baylis did more single-handedly for the British theatre than any other woman in history.

In water one sees one's own face, but in wine one beholds the heart of another.
French Proverb
I never worry about diets. The only carrots that interest me are the number you get in a diamond.
Mae West

Making love without love is like trying to make a soufflé without eggs.
Simone Beck

Every fruit has its secret.
D H Lawrence

CHAPTER NINETEEN

P G Wodehouse

P G Wodehouse was born in Guildford. He wrote about the aristocracy, class distinctions, butlers and gentlemen burglars. Although most of his witty lyrics have been almost forgotten now, they were sung by stars such as Bea Lillie and Gertie Lawrence.

In 1904, Wodehouse became involved with the theatre. He was asked to write an extra lyric for a show in London and his friend Guy Bolton knew he had a good ear for music. As a result of a successful song, the actor Seymour Hicks offered him a job at the Aldwych Theatre as a lyricist to write extra material when needed for a number of musical comedies, and to adapt verses and songs. A friend who was with him at the time said, "On leaving the stage door, Wodehouse was so stunned with joy and excitement that we walked a mile along the Strand without him knowing where he was or whether he was coming or going." The composer he was to work with was Jerome Kern, and thus began a collaboration some years later of Kern and Wodehouse.

Besides *Oh Lady, Lady* there were seven or eight other hit shows including *Oh Boy* (1917) renamed *Oh Joy* in London, with Beatrice Lillie, and *Oh Kay* with Gertie Lawrence. George and Ira Gershwin wrote the music and lyrics for this one but they wrote the book and also part of *Anything Goes*. *Oh Kay* was a hit on both sides of the Atlantic.

It is interesting to note the way he worked with Jerome Kern. Wodehouse said that Jerome usually wrote the music first and then he would add the words. That way he can see which are the musical high spots in it, and can fit the high spots to the lyric. W S Gilbert, of Gilbert and Sullivan fame argued with this and said the words should come first. Wodehouse's talent was not in writing lyrics that read as light verse but fitting the words to the tune.

Unfortunately these musical comedies are no longer produced, but Broadway still remembers those hits. Ira Gershwin, Cole Porter, Noel Coward all recognised his unique style, although hardly any of his lyrics survived.

Wodehouse was criticised for being in America during the 1914–1918 war; however, he had trouble with his eyes, which excused him although his public did not know this fact. His greatest successes were in New York in the 1920s, and people such as Noel

Coward and Gertie Lawrence would have been vastly impressed with the huge successes he was having. He crossed the Atlantic frequently, to enable him to work on the productions both in New York and London.

His nickname was Plum, and in January 1929 his daughter wrote an article about him for the *Strand Magazine*, saying that he had an overwhelming horror of being bored, and an overpowering hatred of hurting people.

It is unusual that a writer whose subjects seem so much attuned to British readers should have so much success in America. However, the Americans have always had an interest in British writing. The common language, the fact that historically the Americans were of British stock, and the traditional colonial inferiority complex made many of them consider work emanating from England superior to what was written in the United States. The turn-of-the-century habit of US heiresses marrying English aristocrats is another example of this veneration of their English roots.

Wodehouse might have appealed because his writing is a put-down of English superiority; his aristocrats are buffoons, his Jeeves is like Barrie's Admirable Crichton, in that he is cleverer, more realistic than his master. Wooster's London club, The Drones, for example, is not one that an intelligent American would aspire to. In fact the whole English social scene is farcical, a sort of never-never land of unmerited affluence and ease, with trivial pre-occupations and pointless activities conducted by mindless idiots, condescended to by their servants.

His style has been often praised to the skies; it is simple, clear, direct and witty in a school-boyish way. In fact in England, his greatest fans have been schoolboys, many of whom carried their infatuation into their adult lives. George Bernard Shaw, who was neither English nor a public-school product, had little regard for Wodehouse's work, any more than he did for another schoolboy favourite, G K Chesterton. Both Chesterton and Wodehouse were enormously popular with the English middle classes, though neither had written anything remotely intellectual, or, dare one say it, intelligent.

Bertie Wooster is the prototype of the genre of idle young men, living on inherited wealth or allowances from family fortunes, who had nothing worthwhile to do, nor any interest in doing anything worthwhile. Wodehouse's genius was in making such a person a subject for comedy, and his trivial preoccupations, dress, parties and other social engagements, comic. There is no hint of political interest in Wodehouse, he is not even satirical, and his characters, Jeeves and Bertie Wooster, were not drawn from living models; Lord Emsworth is similarly an imaginary but comic figure, with his obsession with a pig. So it is easy now to understand why he was drawn into recording messages for broadcasting from Germany to America during the Second World War.

The Royal Court Theatre in London still has the reputation of producing new and often very controversial plays. It was the theatre where John Osborne's *Look Back in Anger* was first produced, and the era of the Angry Young Man and the Kitchen Sink Drama began.

Wodehouse Poem

In the usual Fleet-street garret
Sat a poet; and the Parrot,
Full of quaint misinformation,
Fluttering idly through the door,
Found him dashing off a sonnet.
He was gently musing on it,
When the Parrot broke the silence
With "Your food will cost you more!"

Said the bard, "Ah, pray be quiet!
What have I to do with diet
When the myst'ries of Parnassus
I am trying to explore?
With this aim my soul obsessing
I consider it depressing,
This degrading, fleshly question
Whether food will cost us more.

"I consume not steak nor chop. I
Take a lily or a poppy,
And I gaze on it, enraptured,
Every day from one to four.
Insignificant my bill is
For a day's supply of lilies.
Now I hope you understand why
Food can never cost me more."

Oscar Wilde said...

It is very vulgar to talk about one's business. Only people like stockbrokers do that, and then merely at dinner parties.

Education is an admirable thing, but it is well to remember from time to time that nothing that is worth knowing can be taught.

Experience is the name every one gives to their mistakes.

Relations are simply a tedious pack of people, who haven't got the remotest knowledge of how to live, nor the smallest instinct about when to die.

When I ask for a watercress sandwich, I do not mean a loaf with a field in the middle of it.

CHAPTER TWENTY

Following in Noel Coward's Footsteps

In 1999, a Gala was organised at the Savoy Hotel to celebrate the centenary of Noel Coward's birth. Most of the room was full of thespians and his devotees. Coward illustrates both an era and a type, by means of his music, his plays and his own persona. His name conjures up a mental image of cigarette holders, silk dressing gowns and Riviera balconies, his music is an evocation of England between the wars; think of "The Stately Homes of England", "Dance Little Lady", "A Room with a View", "Don't Put Your Daughter on the Stage" and so on.

His familiarity with the great stars of the theatre and aristocratic society is a tribute to his ambition, his extraordinary talent and upward mobility. He had been however born in an unfashionable suburb of London to lower-middle-class parents who had to turn their home into a lodging house. His mother early on recognised Noel's talents and became a typical stage mother, and without any theatrical background herself strongly encouraged and helped Noel to realise his potential.

In 1930, at the height of his career, Noel moved out of his parents' house to his own far more fashionable establishment at 17 Gerald Road where he loved to give big, often rowdy parties attended by personalities such as Laurence Olivier and Vivien Leigh, Ivor Novello, John Gielgud, Joan Crawford, Douglas Fairbanks Jnr, Lord Amherst, Lord Louis Mountbatten and the then Duke of Kent. The house itself was decorated by Somerset Maugham's wife Syrie, whose panache as an interior decorator was intensified by her love of white on white, or white and black, a style characteristic of the pre-war period.

While probably best known for his witty brittle society comedies, he expressed his patriotism in works such as *Cavalcade* and *In Which We Serve*. It was therefore all the more difficult for him to be attacked for lack of patriotism when he went to live in Switzerland and Jamaica to avoid the punitive taxation of the post-war years, a move he was able to make thanks to a new career as a cabaret star in America, both in the relatively new medium of television and on stage. This cabaret work had come about partly as a result of his introducing Marlene Dietrich to post-war cabaret audiences. The deciding factor, however, was not so much professional pride but more the financial attractions. Las Vegas, which loved his over-the-top Englishness and thrilled to his racy rendition of Cole Porter's "Let's Do It, Let's Fall In Love", paid him a small fortune each week for the privilege of hearing "Mad Dogs and Englishmen".

Although he was to return to England to work, he was, from the early 1950s, an exile. True, he had the rare privilege of enjoying a critical re-evaluation within his own lifetime, largely thanks to his old protégé, Laurence Olivier, asking him to direct *Hay Fever* at the National Theatre in 1964.

Despite his remarkable work on behalf of the war effort from 1939 to 1945, that saw him tour the Empire giving innumerable concerts to battle-weary troops, and above all despite his superb film, *In Which We Serve*, which immortalised the exploits of his friend, Lord Louis Mountbatten, and despite the immediate post-war success of *Brief Encounter*, Coward fell out of critical favour. This, combined with the exigencies of post-war taxation, led him to seek work, and a home, overseas.

He is buried where he died, in his holiday home in Jamaica. This was partly a romantic gesture—like Robin Hood, he had asked to be buried wherever he died—and partly a symbol of the peace that he had found in that beautiful, lush, Caribbean countryside with its view of one of the great loves of his life, the open sea. And yet one cannot help but feel that his choice was also a silent and everlasting reproach to his homeland for waiting until he was seventy before giving him the knighthood that he had so clearly earned a quarter of a century before. Perhaps if the persecution and shame that he had always feared, as a homosexual, had not been so viciously visited on friends and acquaintances who shared his sexuality, if his success had not been envied and his popularity so easily dismissed by "highbrow" critics, then he might well have been laid to rest among his own people, and in the city he loved so much. He would have been pleased to know that a plaque to his memory was laid in the splendid surroundings of Westminster Abbey, but I am sure he would have preferred above all else to have been able to continue to share his hospitality and his home in Gerald Road, where "what has been in past forgetting".

Most of his plays were presented at the Phoenix Theatre in Charing Cross Road, and this was where his seventieth-birthday celebrations was held, attended by well-known theatre personalities as well as by Princess Margaret and Lord Snowdon.

The bar in the Phoenix Theatre is dedicated to his memory, and contains many photographs of him.

To follow actually in his footsteps, you would have only to go from the Phoenix Theatre down to the Ivy Restaurant, his favourite spot for lunch, or carry on down to the Savoy Grill at the Savoy Hotel. In his poem, "The Boy Actor", he wrote a line about walking down The Strand holding his mother's hand after attending an audition as a very young man.

He also frequented Rules in Maiden Lane and Simpson's-in-the-Strand.

CHAPTER TWENTY-ONE

Robert Morley

Robert Morley, actor, author and playwright was born in the British Isles in 1908. He has starred in thirty-seven films as well as being featured in various stage roles. Some of the films he appeared in include *The African Queen*, *The Road to Hong Kong*, *Those Magnificent Men in Their Flying Machines*, *Hotel Paridiso*, *Major Barbara*, *Beat the Devil*, and many, many more. Morley is also an accomplished writer of books as well as various magazine and newspaper articles. Here is an extract from his work:

A feast can be whatever you make it, wherever you enjoy yourself: lugging hampers stuffed with goodies to join the guns, or pocketing a few Marmite sandwiches for yourself and friend to be eaten on Paddington station in the intervals of writing down engine numbers. A feast can be the first fling when you stop going Dutch at the cafe and manfully pick up her bill as well as your own; or the last, with the table loaded with the funeral baked meats, and your friends telling each other how much you would have enjoyed the whole thing if only you'd been there. But, of course, you are.

I have left instructions for caviare and champagne. If there is one thing I and, I sense, the country is determined to avoid at all cost, it is the final extravagance of death duties.

Afternoon Tea Now Being Served

How perfectly Oscar Wilde understood the importance of afternoon tea. There is a line in one of his plays about the dearth of cucumbers for the sandwiches which wrings the heartstrings. "No cucumbers, Lane?" "Not even for ready money, sir." I have always been devoted to afternoon tea, an afternoon without it seems purposeless, and yet quite often these days I have to go without. Not at home, of course, there is always tea at home, but without guests and especially grandchildren, the fare tends to sparseness, and more often than not the butter has not been left out of the refrigerator. Why cannot anyone design a reasonable compartment for the butter where it doesn't freeze to death? I sometimes look at the advertisements for soft margarine and wonder whether it's worth a try. Tea, then, for what it's worth, at home is flapjacks or crumpets, shortcake and gingerbread, Swiss roll and chocolate biscuits and one or two cakes which need eating up. On Sundays and feast days when we sit round the dining-room table with the family it's altogether a more elaborate affair, with ginger snaps filled with cream and playmate biscuits and cucumber and pâté sandwiches and scones and jam, and the cakes of course are fresh, like the brown bread.

Ah well, having declared my interest in tea, as they say these days, or are supposed to say, let's venture further afield and contemplate how seriously this beautiful meal is taken by the catering trade as a whole. High praise to start with to the Savoy where I once gave a tea party to about twenty guests and was allotted a private sitting-room, two waiters and maitre d'hotel who processed around with tea and cream and milk on silver trays and offered poached eggs in muffins and five sorts of sandwiches and mille feuilles and chocolate cake. Just about right, and of course a butler at the tea table makes all the difference. In Kent when I was young there were Sunday teas under a cedar tree and cake stands carried in procession across the lawn and silver trays, and large cups for the gentlemen and small for the ladies. They were not my teacups or my footmen, but for the rest of the week selling vacuum cleaners from doorstep to doorstep I would hug the memory of gracious living and Dundee cake.

Since the War, things have never been quite the same. Two who never survived the holocaust were Fuller's Walnut Cake and Sainsbury's Breakfast Sausage. I count myself fortunate that in my formative years, and indeed for some time afterwards, I ate my share of both. But tea shops are not what they were, particularly down South, though there is one opposite Kew Gardens which specialises in Maids-of-Honour, and Fortnum's still does its duty nobly. Indeed, their restaurant off Jermyn Street with its soda fountain is open unexpectedly late in the evenings in case you've missed out earlier, and there is deep consolation to be found in one of their elegant rarebits washed down with a chocolate milk shake.

Do my readers remember, as I do, Gunter's in Berkeley Square and Stewart's in Piccadilly, and the Trocadero in Shaftesbury Avenue? One is tempted to ask what on earth people do in the afternoon these days. Of course, there is always the Ritz.

In an endeavour to find out what happened to the trade I looked up tea shops in the Yellow Pages, to find the sole listing of such establishments is now confined to Capone, A., 38 Churton Street, S.W.1. I rang up to enquire about reserving a table, but something in my voice alerted the member of the staff who answered.

"You won't like it much here," he told me, "this is a tea-room for working men and we don't reserve."

A similar enquiry to Gunter's, now in Bryanston Street, provided a more puzzling response. Tea was apparently available as long as I knew Mr. Vincent, who was out at the moment. I said I looked forward to meeting him and would it be all right if I brought a friend? The voice raised no objection and asked for the name and initial and when I'd given it, the time.

"I thought about four," I said.

"And you're a friend of Mr. Vincent's?" Again the fatal enquiry.

"Not yet, but I hope to be a great friend after tea."

"If you're not a friend already, I don't think you'd better come. Who are you, exactly?"

"A member of the public," I replied with unaccustomed humility.

"We've given up entertaining them," the voice rebuked, and hung up.

I tried Bentinck's, who used to serve tea in Bond Street and Wigmore Street, but now apparently only do so in Sloane Street, and never after five-thirty. Marshall's tea is cleared away by five, as is the custom in most department stores. I feel slightly embarrassed taking tea where I am not proposing to shop or spend the night. It was not always thus. Hotels especially used to promote tea time, and Selfridge's Hotel still has a pianist. But what happened to the Gypsy Bands, what happened to the *thes dansants*, what happened to the trios and the quartets of gallant lady musicians who played amid the palms up and down the country from their repertoire of light music? "Two teas with buttered toast, and will you ask them to play something from Lilac Time?" How proud, how happy I used to be when my request was granted; how appreciatively I would smile at the leader and clap all concerned. Dare I ask for the Cobbler's Song from Chu Chin Chow as an encore? I dared.

You will have to go a very long way indeed to recapture such pleasure, but intending travellers to Canada might care to know that in the Chateau Frontenac in Quebec they still strike up in the Palm Court as soon as lunch is over, and that the gentlemen of the ensemble wear wigs not false hair pieces, you understand but genuine period wigs tied with bows. Come to think of it, I enjoyed it more than Niagara.

The Charing Cross Hotel

My family have always been extravagantly fond of the Charing Cross Hotel. My father used to take himself there for brief stays in moments of financial crisis, and as these were by no means infrequent, spent a good deal of time there trying to raise the wind and avoid the creditors. My sister still meets her friends there after shopping excursions from Kent, favouring the upstairs bar and tea lounge away from the commuters who crowd the downstairs ones, bracing themselves after a relaxed day at the office for the domestic encounter which has to come when the six-thirty-eight arrives, as it inevitably must, sometime, at Bexley Halt. At home there is no one to fall back upon, no secretary to iron out the crumples. At home we are all equal, each expected to pull his weight, to mend the washing machine, to speak firmly to the children, to mow the grass. Nevertheless the Charing Cross, like all London station hotels, is a cheerful place round about six-thirty in the evening: it has not perhaps the excitement of the Grosvenor at Victoria where the train to catch might just possibly not be stopping at Bognor Regis but going straight through to Budapest. Nor has it quite the "I'm alright Jack" atmosphere of the Great

Western Hotel where the drinks tend to be large Gin and Tonics and the conversation about either the week-end just past or the one to come. If there was anything so vulgar as a polo "crowd", these are your puckachuka people.

No one, as far as I know, plays polo in Kent. They are far more politically minded, even at times electing Liberals. When they are not canvassing each other or voting they are carrying large trays of mushrooms down to the garden gate and selling them to passing motorists along with seasonal fruit and chicken manure. Kent is the original blackboard jungle and some of the profits find their way back to the Charing Cross Hotel. The dining-room retains the original decor, all green and pink and chaste nymphs censored from the waist down but with bust well to the fore, as might be expected of any goddess supporting a ceiling on her shoulders. There is a pianist strumming "I Want To Be Happy" and "Tea for Two", and a lot of space between the tables.

On the night I was there for an early dinner the customers didn't crowd each other either. Elderly couples whose lifetime habits were well known to each other: "Madam will have a glass of Chablis—you do have it by the glass, don't you—and for myself a pint of light ale to start with." Anything in quotes in this chapter is word for word, by the way. I have recently purchased, or to be more accurate, had lent to me with an option to purchase, a hearing aid, and I now hear perfectly what is going on around me. I can hear knives clatter, plates being scraped, people chewing, paper rustling, my own bones creaking; what I can't hear accurately is what is being said to me. Do I like the unaccustomed sounds of my own private Watergate? I am still not sure. I went to the theatre after dinner and heard every word for once, but then for once everyone spoke up.

But to return to the Charing Cross Hotel. The food was good on the whole, the melon rather old-fashioned and sliced; I disapprove of sliced melon but I suppose it's one of the first things they teach in the kitchens of the culinary schools. No doubt it makes the melon look a bit gayer, especially when they spear a cherry and put it on the top. Gone are the days when fruit knives were made of silver, and steel was not supposed to touch fruit. My wife and I both had Wiener Schnitzels. I have promised myself that for once I will be factual; there is a charm I always think in reading what the writer and his companion actually ate. When, as often happens, the new overwhelms when cricket pitches are wilfully destroyed and no one has the courage to carry the stumps and bails a few yards and set them up on another piece of the ground, then naked men leap the wicket and row around on park ponds, when the Burtons come together again and the world holds its breath or merely lets it out in one long expiring gasp, it is comforting, surely, to read that my wife chose fruit salad and I had a chocolate eclair of immense excellence and regretted not having accepted the offer of another. We didn't order coffee but it came just the same. The bill took its time, and by then we were anxious not to miss the curtain. The pianist played "My Heart Stood Still" as we walked out On the whole, as it turned out, it would have been wiser to linger and let him complete his repertoire: the play was God-awful.

Hoping for once to get ahead of my colleagues, I accepted an invitation recently to fly the Concorde all the way to Gander and back one fine summer morning and sample breakfast at twice the speed of sound and lunch at precisely the same pace. A feature of the dining-room, indeed of the cabin, is an illuminated computer sign which records the rate of sky hurtle. Whether it is the same reading as the captain takes, of course, one doesn't know for certain, as you don't even pass a cloud at fifty thousand feet. The food was brisk and hot, and for breakfast there was the customary sausages, kidney, steak, mushroom, tomato and sauté potatoes, followed and preceded by champagne, a good claret, a fair white burgundy, a really delicious trifle, coffee and liqueurs.

By the time we had explored Gander—something of a ghost airport these days, alas— it was time to be thinking of getting back and luncheon. Meals will come thick and fast on the Concorde, apparently. It took two and a half hours to cross the Atlantic once more, just time for cocktails, canapés, ham stuffed with foie gras and supreme of chicken, excellent cheese, and fruit salad iced with brandy. The wines were the same as at breakfast. The speed seems fairly constant; either the pilot was chicken or for some reason unable to raise the speed to three times that of sound, I am not sure which. No doubt it will come.

Supersonic food will come too, and quickly; in theory there is perhaps little point in man pressing his luck but in practice he usually does.

Faced with the choice of crossing to New York in a leisurely jumbo and a chance for another look at *Gone With The Wind* and an elaborate bouquet (at any rate in the first class), or a quick streak across the waves in less than half the time, I think we will all go for the streak. I don't know why; it isn't as if there was a great deal to do when we got there, but we like to think there is. There was nothing whatever to do in Gander but buy terracotta statues of Newfoundland fishermen. Even my small grand-daughter, the keenest of magpies, left it behind after we had reached home for tea.

Oscar Wilde said…

Don't talk to me about the weather…Whenever people talk to me about the weather, I always feel quite certain that they mean something else.

One should never trust a woman who tells one her real age. A woman who would tell one that, would tell one anything.

Work is the curse of the drinking classes.

I never travel without my diary. One should always have something sensational to read in the train.

CHAPTER TWENTY-TWO

Judy Campbell
"Everyone needs Jam"

This is a poem written for Judy Campbell by Clemence Dane while they were waiting to be served at the Ivy early in 1942

> Oh Judy, Judy, here comes Spring
> In gown in green and gold
> The early lark is on the wing
> The daffodils and violets sing
> Oh Judy, there will be a Spring
> When even Judy's old.

Judy Campbell, an actress who originated the female lead with Noel Coward in several of his plays was interviewed for his centenary celebration in 1999. She is a legend in her own time and especially as the singer who introduced the song "A Nightingale Sang in Berkeley Square" and made it her own.

She tells the story of how she first met Coward at the Savoy Grill, and he auditioned her on the spot for a part in one of his plays.

A short time later, he invited her to lunch at the Ivy. During the meal she told him all about her work and what she had been doing. At the end of the lunch, he said, "And what about the jam?"

"What jam?" she asked, wondering if it was a new dessert.

Coward said that she had told him all about her news and what was happening in her life, but she had said nothing, or showed no interest in his work. She immediately replied that she thought that he was far too successful and much too busy to expect any compliments or interest from her.

"Not at all," he replied, "everybody needs jam!"

She never forgot his advice, and even though she toured all over England with him, he ended up "not liking me very much at all because I went away, got married and had children so that was that". Judy wrote one chapter in Graham Payne's *My Life with Noel Coward*, and she and Graham were at the Ivy for the launch of his book together with most of the theatrical profession who were free to go.

The wonderful thing about Judy is her willingness to take part in anything that's going on. From charity galas, revues to poetry readings she always says, "Yes."

Another wonderful actress still going strong is Margaret Towner who is the mother of the actor/artist/cartoonist Clive Francis. She brilliantly portrayed the wardrobe mistress in the play of the same name which was produced at the King's Head Theatre in London. Her great contribution was to add some speeches of her own recounting the great performances she had seen at the Old Vic.

Wardrobe mistresses very rarely "get any jam", even though their work is indispensable in any production. Here is a poem by John Ferguson written in 1912.

The Wardrobe Mistress

Saddened by dreams of what she might have been,
Sick with the thought of what she is today,
She droops, a little woman, pinched and gray,
Within the shadow of a painted scene;
Still lingers on her weary face the sheen
Of make-believe; the cruel crow's-feet stray
Beneath her faded eyes, and mute dismay
Lurks in her timid and pathetic mien.

Echoes of by-gone triumphs wake her breast
The nights of tinselled bliss, the dizzy whirl,
The sparkling gauds, the limelight and the band
Now with a needle in her work-worn hand,
She potters round the wings, all drably drest,
Stitching the trappings of some thoughtless girl.

Oscar Wilde said...

A man cannot be too careful in the choice of his enemies.

The English have a miraculous power of turning wine into water.

CHAPTER TWENTY-THREE

Judi Dench

Dame Judi started her career during the golden era in the West End. She followed in the footsteps of Sybil Thorndike, Edith Evans, Peggy Ashcroft, Coral Brown. Now she has come into her own, as one of England's top classical actresses. Her work is seen by millions across the world in film, on television and on the stage, and she acts both on Broadway and in London.

Dame Judi is the epitome of grace. Not only in her work, but off stage as well. Many actresses are difficult both off stage and on, but Judi charms just about everybody. She was presented with the Sir John Gielgud Award for Excellence in the Dramatic Arts by the Shakespeare Guild, at the Barrymore Theatre in New York in 1999. The award itself was the Golden Quill. Judi told her biographer John Miller "They're keeping me in the dark about what's actually going to happen. I think it's scenes from Shakespeare, and I believe Richard Eyre and David Hare are doing a cabaret act."

Christopher Plummer began the evening's tribute. "I was lucky enough to be in the same Company as Judi Dench, the Royal Shakespeare Company in London and Stratford-upon-Avon. What a formidable company it was that year. Not only were the senior alumni represented by John Gielgud and Dame Peggy Ashcroft, but each one of the leading younger members of the company became a star in his or her own right. A young Sir Peter Hall, a young Franco Zeffirelli, a young Colin Blakeley, Ian Bannen, Christopher Plummer—what a cast ! And the leading ladies—a hilarious Geraldine McEwan, a magical Dorothy Tutin, a wondrously young Vanessa Redgrave and, youngest of all, a pert, delectable, talented, enchanting Judi Dench."

She was already in tears by the time he ended with a poem to her and was relieved when the auditorium was darkened for the screening of two scenes from *Mrs Brown*. Hal Holbrook followed with a speech by Shylock, happily unaware that it was from Judi's least favourite Shakespeare play.

Richard Eyre spoke of how the one quality Judi has never seemed to need is luck: "…but for we mortals who need it badly, and who have become her friends, and who have worked with her, she has been part of our luck."

Later that evening she stood and shook hands with over two hundred people who wanted to congratulate her, while her well-earned dinner turned cold on the table behind her. The receiving line kept up for over an hour and she delighted everybody. In his biography of Judi, John Miller tells of her total dedication to a production she is working on.

Judi has her regular routine when working in a play. She is usually one of the first of the actors to arrive at the theatre. She has a cup of tea with honey in it, and later on she takes a little phial of ginseng and royal jelly. She says it's just like drinking pure honey, and she takes it before each performance, matinee and evening.

"I wouldn't feel right if I didn't have that." The energy needed to get through a long part is enormous, and she used to go out for tea between a matinee and an evening show, but during the run of *Amy's View* on Broadway, she found that she needed to sleep instead.

During the run of *Amy's View* at the Barrymore, the crew would grill a barbecue lunch every Sunday in the back lot behind the theatre, and the cast would bring contributions to the buffet.

In 1999 she was the first actress to win both an Oscar and a Tony in the same year since Ellen Burstyn twenty years before.

But, as Miller writes, "Awards matter less to Judi than parts." Just before she left for America she received an invitation from Trevor Nunn to return to the National Theatre in a particular play that lacked appeal for her. She replied, "I want to come back to the National, but not in that part. Would you ask me to do something more frightening than that?"

There can be little doubt that he will, nor that Peter Hall, Richard Eyre and many others will not be far behind. She will certainly make more films—the offers are now pouring in—and she will continue to appear on television and radio, but we can rest assured that she will not deny us the chance to see and hear her in her natural habitat—the stage.

Judi's favourite recipe for cooking the perfect salmon:

> Sprinkle salmon with a little lemon juice and freshly-ground black pepper. Wrap in foil and lower into boiling water, in a fish kettle if you have one. Cover it and cook for three minutes only. Take pan off heat and put in cool place. When the water is just hand-hot the salmon is cooked. Serve with Hollandaise sauce.

Her favourite London restaurant is Zillis in Soho, which she says makes the best lobster ravioli she has ever eaten.

Most actors have their "comfort" food, although the term is little known in the States. Judi has her cup of tea with honey in it, and I asked David Suchet when he was on Broadway playing Salieri in *Amadeus* what his was. "Corned beef hash with a fried egg on top."

"Something eggy on toast on a tray" was what Noel Coward liked when he was confined to bed with a cold or exhaustion.

During the run of my anthology *Love from Shakespeare to Coward* I would rehearse the actors in my flat in Covent Garden, and during the break I would serve them tea and cinnamon toast, a comfort food for dark wintry afternoons. The secret is to sprinkle sugar as well as cinnamon on the hot toast that melts into the butter. Most of the actors would then tell me all about their own comfort food, and it nearly always involved toast. Comfort foods can also include desserts of course; rice pudding and trifle are two of the most favourite, and also "Spotted Dick", a steamed pudding with raisins, which dates back to the days of Charles Dickens. And, of course, custard tarts are the favourite of Lionel's (played by Geoffrey Palmer) in the TV series *As Time Goes By* starring Judi Dench.

Caroline Lange, an actress friend of mine, wrote the following poem after a friend of hers had an unhappy affair with a married man. She imagines her friend speculating about his wife, her competitor.

The Wife

Is she dark? Is she fair?
Or has she greying, thinning hair?
Is she tall, smart and slim?
Or short and dumpy, with double chin?
Is she blessed with ten green fingers?
Is her perfume one that lingers?
Does she excel at Spotted Dick?
And eggs and bacon in a tick?
Wafer thin bread and butter?
Is her kitchen free from clutter?
Is she very loving when you cuddle up at
    night?
Does she put her hair in curlers? What a
    ghastly sight!
I wonder what she wears in bed? Chanel
    No 5?
A whiff of heady perfume increases sexual
    drive.
Is she plain? Is she pretty?

Is she dull? Or bright and witty?
I wonder if her teeth are false?
I have all my own, of course!
Are her stockings made of lyle?
I'm sure she hasn't any style!
I know I sound an awful cow
But where on earth do I go now?
Her problem is she's not like me!
All that anti-wrinkle cream is really not
    much fun!
I bet she's overweight! I bet she weighs a
    ton!
I've decided that I've had enough, the whole
thing makes me sick!
I've decided he can keep his wife
—and her spotted Dick!

*With permission: Caroline
Lange*

CHAPTER TWENTY-FOUR

Celebrity recipes

Most drama students would agree that besides getting their Equity card and their first job, the next success in becoming a professional actor is joining The National or the RSC and to be able to afford to dine with friends in Rules, the Caprice, the Ivy or the Savoy, and wave to their fellow thespians who too are ready to follow in the footsteps of the famous. But while they're waiting they can always try some of these recipes!

Theatre

The theatre is a world apart
No matter what they say.
It has a different kind of heart,
A different kind of day.
It tells of things you dare not tell,
Of ages passed away,
Of Heaven, Earth and deepest Hell,
Of work and love and play.
It's all tied up with sex and death,
With comedy and strife,
And the magic of the human past
The theatre brings to life.
In fact as long as men have minds
And hearts that sometimes break,
They'll always leave the mundane street
To see the gods awake...

Menus are like programs,
The Curtain is up!
First act, first course, first laugh!
Poetry, pleasure, a feast of words,
Appetites quicken as we await the start.

Nicholas Smith

Tripes Lyonnaises

1lb of Tripe	*1oz of Fat for frying*
3 Onions	*Stock and Seasoning*

Wash and clean the tripe (removing surplus fat). Cut into finger-length strips 1/2 inch wide. Slice onions and fry brown. Remove from the pan and fry tripe brown. Place tripe and onions in a casserole with stock and seasoning (water with a little Marmite or Worcester sauce will do.) Put on lid and cook in a slow oven for 2½ hours.

Garnish with chopped parsley. Serve with potatoes baked in the oven.

Sole Matelote

Remove the dark skin and lay the fish in a greased fireproof dish, skinned side down. Half cover the fish with cider and water mixed in equal quantities. Dust over with salt and decorate with sprigs of parsley at the sides.

Cook in a moderate oven 375° for twenty minutes or a little less according to the size of the sole.

Then remove the parsley and thicken the liquid with a piece of butter—about 2 oz.— and two teaspoonfuls of flour, mixed very smoothly. Pour over fish, and sprinkle very fine brown breadcrumbs over it. Replace parsley.

Blanquette de Veau

Trim veal of fat, cut into small pieces and place in a pan with sliced onions and carrots, browned lightly in butter. Then add cold water to cover and simmer for two to three hours. Add two bay leaves.

Boil in a separate saucepan trimmings from veal, three bacon rinds (tied with string), salt, pepper, a pinch of herbs and half an onion. Simmer for one hour. Then prepare small button onions, cut carrots into fancy shapes and cook in this stock. (Add a few mushrooms if liked). Allow to cool.

Now pour off the stock from the veal and thicken it with flour and cold water, season with celery, salt and pepper. Add one large tablespoonful of sherry and simmer for twenty minutes. Strain stock. Beat yolk of an egg, add a little cream and add to strained stock. Heat gently but be careful it does not boil. Pour sauce over the veal and garnish with the carrots and onions which have been drained.

Serve with the creamiest of mashed potatoes and the newest of peas and with it drink a light, very cold white wine.

19 *Right: Rules: public door on left, door for Royalty on right.*

20 *Below left: Margaret Thatcher at Rules.*

21 *Below right: the Greene Room. Graham Greene, who spent much of his life in the south of France, still chose to spend all of his birthdays in the Rules. It features in several of his books and letters from Greene and his sister Elizabeth are displayed on the walls of the Greene Room.*

22   *Charles Dickens Room at Rules.*

23   *The entrance to the Charles Dickens Room.*

24 *Above: Rules: caricature of Sir Noel Coward.*

25 *Below left: The alcove where Edward VII entertained the actress Lily Langtree.*

26 *Below right: Interior of John Betjeman Room.*

27 *Sir John Gielgud's favourite table at Rules.*

28 *Launch of the first book in this series at Rules. Left to right: Judy Campbell (Noel Coward's leading la*
in Present Laughter*), Elizabeth Sharland, Barry J Mishon (enterpreneur/impresario), David Drummon*
(owns the shop Pleasures of Times Past in Cecil Court) and Frank Middlemass (actor).

REX HARRISON

Smoked Tongue

1 smoked Tongue	1 teaspoonful Pepper
6 Bay leaves	1 teaspoonful Cloves
1 sliced Onion	

Cover the tongue with cold water and bring slowly to the boil. Skim well, simmer for 4 hours. Take carefully out and remove the root. Take the skin off.

Arrange on a dish surrounded with whole carrots and spinach, serve with caper sauce.

Caper Sauce

Melt a large knob of butter in a heavy saucepan. Stir in enough flour to absorb the butter. Add enough milk and the strained stock of the tongue to make a thick cream, season to taste. Add well-drained capers, a squeeze of lemon, and if possible a tablespoonful of cream—or stir in at the last moment, away from the heat, a beaten yolk of egg.

SIR LEWIS CASSON

Stew

"I can still boil an egg or even fry one, but otherwise I haven't cooked since the 1914 war, when I hewed a side of frozen beef with an axe and stewed it in dixies over a trench fire ... ."

Take equal parts of beef, veal and pork, 2 or 3 onions, 2 or 3 potatoes, lard, paprika, lemon juice.

Slice the onions, cook in fat until brown. Add the meat cut into small pieces.

When brown add enough water (hot) to cover. Add salt and pepper, squeeze of lemon juice and teaspoonful of paprika.

Simmer gently for 2 hours with cover on. Add potatoes sliced, serve when potatoes are done.

A tablespoonful of port or claret added to the sauce just before serving does a lot for this mixture.

CHRISTOPHER FRY

Soufflé Surprise

Thaw a packet of frozen strawberries or raspberries, sprinkle them with castor sugar and brandy and let them stand for awhile.

Then place them in the bottom of a soufflé dish, and fill the dish with slightly softened vanilla ice cream. Cover the top with the stiffly whipped whites of two (better three) eggs to which castor sugar has been added. Brown in a very hot oven and serve at once.

NOEL COWARD

Warsaw Concerto

Eggs   *Breadcrumbs*
Onions   *Butter*
Vinegar   *Seasoning*

Cut the onions into thin slices and fry in butter until brown. Add a little vinegar and continue frying for three to five minutes. Grease a fireproof dish and line with onions.

Slide in the required number of eggs, unbroken, add salt and pepper and cover generously with breadcrumbs.

Dab top with bits of butter and grated cheese. Bake in hot oven for five to six minutes, when eggs should have set.

JUDY CAMPBELL

Fish Soufflé for Beginners

¾ lb of cooked Fish   *2 oz. of Butter*
    (preferably   *2 eggs*
    Finnan Haddock)   *½ pint of Milk*
    1 large tablespoonful of Flour

Melt the butter, mix in the flour smoothly, add the milk very slowly (as for making white sauce). Stir well until boiling.

Add the flaked fish. Take the pan off the heat and beat in the yolks of 2 eggs, whisk the whites of eggs and fold into the mixture. Pour into a greased soufflé dish in moderate oven for about half an hour. Eat at once.

IVOR NOVELLO

Chicken Mornay

Boil a chicken in the usual way. Skin; take the meat off the bone and cut into small pieces; arrange in a baking dish with some chopped bacon (or ham). Add a small glass of white wine, salt and pepper. Let chicken simmer in the wine for ten minutes.

Make a rich white sauce, using cream if possible (or top of milk). Stir in as much grated cheese as you can spare. Add the sauce to the chicken. Cover the top with Post Toasties, a few knobs of butter, and brown in oven.

This was Ivor Novello's favourite recipe; it was originally contributed by his chef at Redroofs.

DAME SYBIL THORNDIKE

Stew

"I'm no cook, I make stews and porridge; and usual everyday stew is the thing I suppose. Here goes:

Take anything that's left over, fry it all up with more vegetables of any or every sort, put any flavouring you like (Worcester Sauce by me preferred), cook and cook and cook till it's a gorgeous mess. And if you don't like it I've no use for you at all: for it's lovely.

EVELYN LAYE

Southern Fried Chicken

Choose a young bird, a roaster. Skin the breast and cut it up into sections, add pepper and salt, put them in a bowl of milk. (This is very important as it helps to make it tender.) Leave them to soak for two hours.

Take the pieces out of the milk, dry them and then roll them in flour which has been salt and peppered.

Have a deep frying-pan of pure fat at boiling point (to fry them in butter is the ideal). Cook the dark meat first, rather fiercely, then the white meat (so that it is sealed), then turn the heat low and allow the chicken to cook gently for about an hour. Turning the pieces from time to time.

When taking the chicken out of the fat drain it well on to a sheet of greaseproof paper.

Serve it with rashers of crisply fried bacon and little balls made of sweetcorn bound with white sauce and fried.

Serve with salad.

TERENCE RATTIGAN

Little Chickens stuffed with Cucumber in White Wine Sauce

Choose four even-sized poussins, prepare for toasting. Rub breasts with lemon juice.

Peel a cucumber, remove centre and pips, cut into very small pieces. Chop finely one rasher of lean bacon, mix with cucumber, add a cupful of white breadcrumbs and season well with salt and pepper. Bind with an egg.

Stuff the birds carefully with the cucumber forcemeat and roast them (if possible in butter) basting frequently. Ten minutes before the birds are done, pour over them a glass of white wine. Baste once or twice again.

Serve the birds on fried bread with the juice from the roasting tin poured over them. The gravy can be thickened with a little sieved flour.

ALICIA MARKOVA

Steak Diane

Trim a very thin slice of beef steak of all fat (beat it thin with roller if necessary) and marinate for one hour. (Leave to soak in oil, mixed herbs and finely chopped shallot.)

At end of hour, dry steak thoroughly. Melt a lump of butter in a heavy frying-pan, cook teaspoonful of finely chopped shallot and parsley until brown, add one good tablespoonful of Worcester sauce. Put in steak and cook to taste.

The success of this dish depends upon the thinness of the steak and on it being eaten the moment it is cooked.

JOYCE GRENFELL

Ham in Molasses

When you get a tinned ham from America or other generous sources, place the ham in a fire-proof dish, crust it generously with brown sugar and some cloves, and surround it with six or seven tablespoonfuls of molasses. Place in a medium oven and heat very thoroughly, basting frequently.

Serve it in the fireproof dish.

Fresh frozen peas and creamed potatoes go well with it.

HUGH ("BINKIE") BEAUMONT

Port Wine Sauce for Hot Ham

½ cup Brown Sugar
½ cup Sultanas
¼ cup Almonds
   (blanched and
   chopped)
1 tablespoonful
   Red or
Black currant jelly

1 glass of Port Wine
pinch of Cloves
Juice of ½ lemon
1 teaspoonful
   Cornflour
Pepper and Salt to
   taste

Put the sugar, sultanas, jelly, almonds, cloves and lemon juice into a saucepan over a low heat, stirring until the sugar and jelly are melted.

Add the wine, salt and pepper. Mix cornflour with tablespoonful of cold water, add to sauce, boil up and serve.

ROBERT HELPMANN

Chicken à la King

1 cup Cream (top of milk)
1 cup sliced Mushrooms
2 cups diced, cooked minced chicken
1 Pimento cut in thin strips
1 green Pepper
2 yolks of Egg
3 tablespoonfuls Butter

Make white sauce in the usual way, using half cream and half chicken stock.

Sauté the mushrooms and green peppers in butter for ten minutes. Add the chicken to the white sauce, then the pimento, and finally the cooked mushrooms and green peppers. Season with salt and pepper. Simmer for about five minutes stirring all the time.

Take the pan off the stove and add the beaten yolks of the two eggs. Cook one minute more but do not boil.

Serve ad once on slices of freshly-made hot toast, or in vol-au-vent cases.

The eggs are not absolutely necessary, but give an added richness to the sauce. This recipe would be an excellent way of disguising rabbit.

RONALD SQUIRE

Fillet of Veal and Mushroom Sauce

Steam a piece of fillet of veal in a pan with salt, pepper, one tomato and ¼ lb. of chopped mushrooms. (Allow about one hour for 3 lbs. of veal.)

Take the veal out of the pan and put it in a roasting tin and cover with bacon (or ham). Roast until cooked.

Mushroom Sauce

Melt a knob of butter, add flour. When a smooth roux, add the liquor in which the veal is cooked.

(A few more mushrooms may be added if liked.) Cook to a creamy consistency. Add squeeze of lemon and if possible a tablespoonful of cream.

Serve the veal with creamed potatoes and new peas which have been cooked with sugar and a shred of heart of lettuce.

RONALD SHINER

Fish Supper

"This is my favourite supper after the show."

Grill one boneless kipper. A piece of Finnan Haddock steamed in milk and butter. After cooking, place the haddock on top of the kipper, top with an egg and a cube of butter.

FLORENCE DESMOND

Caesar Salad

Use a large bowl and rub the bowl with garlic. Cut one slice of bread, rub with garlic, smear both sides with olive oil and bake in oven. When baked a rich brown, cut into cubes and mix with salad, which is made as follows: 1 lettuce or more, 1 small tin of anchovies, 1 raw egg.

When the salad is mixed with dressing, sprinkle with cheese. The salad dressing comprises: Olive oil, vinegar, salt, pepper, and a dash of Worcester sauce.

Tangy Supper Salad

1 small head Red Cabbage	1 teaspoonful Sugar
1 medium-sized head Green Cabbage	¾ cupful Salad Oil
	¼ cupful of Vinegar
½ teaspoonful dry Mustard	¼ cupful chopped Onion
1/8 teaspoonful Pepper	1 teaspoonful Sugar
2 teaspoonfuls Celery seed	

Grate red and green cabbage coarsely. Toss together lightly. Combine vinegar, onion, mustard, salt, pepper, sugar, oil and celery seed. Shake until thoroughly blended. Add dressing to cabbage and toss lightly.

Serves six.

Roman Pie

Chicken breasts (boiled)	Truffles
Cold Ham	½ pint White Sauce
(and Tongue	Macaroni
if possible)	Parmesan Cheese
Salt and Pepper	Aspic

Put at the bottom of a Pyrex dish a layer of sliced chicken and ham. Cover with white sauce. Then a layer of macaroni (cooked), cover with white sauce. And so on alternately until the dish is nearly filled—finishing with chicken and ham.

Stand dish in a tin of hot water and steam for an hour, then allow to cool.

Make an aspic jelly by melting ½ oz. of gelatine in a little less than a pint of strained chicken stock.

Decorate the top of the chicken with circles of ham and tomato, pour the aspic over it, and set in the refrigerator.

Serve with cucumber and beetroot salad, and rolls of bread and butter filled with mustard and cress.

Emlyn Williams

Yorkshire Pudding

2 heaped tablespoonfuls	Pinch of Salt
Flour (plain)	1 Egg
Cup of Milk and Water	
(water is important to make it light)	

PUT flour in basin with salt, make a well in the centre, break in the egg. Beat well. Add milk and water gradually until it forms a creamy batter.

Allow mixture to stand for at least one hour.

Melt 1 oz. dripping in the baking tin and when quite hot, pour in the batter and bake for about 20 minutes.

Enough for four people.

Wilfred Pickles

CONSTANCE CUMMINGS

Cold Halibut

1 lb of Halibut	Juice of 2 Lemons
1 yolk of Egg	2 tablespoons Sugar
1 teaspoonful Cornflour	1 Onion
	Salt and Pepper

Wash the halibut, place in a pan with just sufficient water to cover it, together with sliced onions, sugar, lemon juice and pepper and salt. Bring to the boil and simmer for 20 minutes. Remove from heat.

Beat the yolk of the egg. Mix the cornflour to make a paste and add the beaten egg to it. Pour the paste over the fish and simmer very gently for another three minutes until it thickens. Leave to cool.

Steak and Kidney Pudding

½ lb. Suet Pastry	1 lb. Beefsteak
1 tablespoonful of Flour	(buttock or skirt)
¼ lb. of Kidney	½ teaspoonful Salt
1 Onion (optional)	½ teaspoonful of
¼ pint Water	Pepper

Line a deep basin, well greased, with suet pastry ½ inch thick. Put the flour with the salt and pepper on a plate, cut the meat into strips 2½ inches long and 1 inch wide, and the fat into very small pieces. Dip each piece of meat in the seasoned flour, place a small piece of fat on the end of each piece, and roll up.

Place these rolls in the basin along with the chopped kidney. Peel the onion and place it whole in the middle of the meat rolls and kidney. Pour the water over. Wet the edge of the suet lining and cover with a round piece of suet, thoroughly seal the edges, cover with greased paper, and steam 3 hours.

Turkey in Celery Sauce

Wash and scrape three or four sticks of celery and put into a pan with salt, a bay leaf and a pinch of mixed herbs. Cover with half milk and half water and cook until the celery is quite tender. Strain off liquid and put aside. Rub celery through fine sieve.

Place in a pan a knob of butter; when melted stir in sufficient sieved flour to absorb. Cook until mixture leaves the sides of the pan. Gradually add the strained stock in which the celery has been cooked, until the sauce is the consistency of thick cream. Now add the sieved celery, beat well with a fork. Season to taste and add ½ teaspoonful lemon juice.

Having already prepared the breast of cooked turkey, by laying it on a fire-proof dish and warming gently through in the oven, chop about a quarter of a cupful of fresh, raw, cleaned celery, chopped very fine. Beat up the yolk of one egg. Take the sauce off the stove, stir in the celery and the egg, and pour over the warmed turkey. Serve with border of creamed potatoes.

Do no reheat sauce or the egg will curdle. The crunchy taste of the uncooked celery in the hot sauce is delicious.

This sauce can be used equally well with cold chicken.

CHAPTER TWENTY-FIVE

A Short History of London Theatre from 1900 to 1970

The twentieth century began with the year 1900, but in theatre as in other aspects of national life, the division between one century and another was arbitrary and, in some ways, misleading. Just as the nineteenth century did not begin until the defeat of Napoleon at Waterloo in 1815, so the twentieth had to wait for the death of Queen Victoria, in January 1901, before the public could feel, in Lord Tennyson's words (from *Morte d'Arthur*) that "the old order changeth, yielding place to new, lest one good custom should corrupt the world".

The hundred years that were to prove the most exciting, and fruitful, since the Shakespearean heyday some three hundred years earlier, began with some well established theatrical figures, still active. Sir Henry Irving, the first actor ever to be knighted, whose elevation to this high rank had simultaneously raised the profile and the reputation of his trade (and turned it, in public eyes, from a trade to a profession) was still on stage, albeit in decline.

For thirty years he had presided over a succession of Shakespearean triumphs and massively popular renditions of classically Victorian melodramas—most notably *The Bells*—at the Lyceum Theatre. A vast and beautiful building with a long and varied history, in Irving's day (from the 1870s to 1902) it was the centre of London's theatrical and social life, the most fashionable playhouse in London, and in many ways the most stimulating.

By the beginning of the new century, however, Irving was long past his prime, his partnership with Ellen Terry a fond memory rather than the blazing display of professional and private passion that had electrified audiences for decades. Among the countless anecdotes told of Henry Irving, one of the wittiest—if a little "racy"—is that told of when he seduced her for the first time.

After leading up to the event over a candlelit dinner, he accompanied her home, where he made his "move" and, realising that she was very happy for him to do so, began to take his clothes off. As he gradually disrobed—gradual being the operative work, as Victorian gentlemen wore far more clothes than their counterparts a hundred years later—she commented on the various parts of his physique that came into view. When he finally finished this gentlemanly striptease, Miss Terry commented unfavourably on the most important area of all.

Most men might have been put off, to say the least, but Irving, whose knowledge of, and love for, Shakespeare's works was second to none, merely chose an appropriate theatrical quote from one of the Tragedies. "Do not worry, my dear," he muttered, "I have come to bury Caesar, not to praise him!"

Irving carried on touring even after he had been forced to leave his beloved Lyceum (which was largely torn down and rebuilt—as has happened more recently, with Apollo Leisure's massive and welcome refurbishment of the quasi-derelict building in 1996). He died in 1905, in Bradford, during a tour of *Becket*, one of his favourite roles, and which had been particularly popular in his heyday, as it tapped into the Victorian delight in muscular, manly Christianity.

"Victorian Values" as they are known were in some ways thrown overboard in the far more raffish, opulent atmosphere of King Edward VII's reign. With his wealthy, self-made friends, his love of France and his love of women, his court was very different from that of Queen Victoria, whose household had been in enforced mourning for the Prince Consort for some forty years.

Edward's tastes included the theatre, and one of his most famous mistresses was Lily Langtry, the "Jersey Lily" (so named after her birthplace), who graced the stage as well as the royal bed. There was another attractive girl called Lily Langtry who also "trod the boards"—albeit in Music Hall and Variety, and the fact that she shared the same name as the king's beautiful mistress cannot have harmed her career.

The king's mistress lived from 1852–1929, the Variety artiste from 1877 to 1865, and their shared named and similar work reflected the confusion that similar or the same names could generate in show business. One of the many changes that the twentieth century was to bring was the creation of the actors' union, Equity, and the rule that professionals should not have exactly the same name.

This book will concentrate on mainstream theatre, but it should be noted here that Music Hall, which was a fundamentally Victorian institution that lasted from the 1840s to the 1920s, was still going strong as the twentieth century dawned, and just a roll-call of the names of the leading stars who were still active in the early 1900s immediately summons up the period: Harry Lauder, Dan Leno (known as the King's Jester after performing before Edward VII in 1901), Marie Lloyd, Ada Reeve, Vesta Tilley, Little Tich, George Robey—even Harry Houdini.

Half a century later, in *Gay's the Word* (with lyrics by Alan Melville) Ivor Novello was to celebrate these stars of his youth with just such a roll-call in *Vitality*, the hit number sung by Cicely Courtneidge, who later used it as her theme song for the rest of her career.

In some ways Edward VII's reign seemed a triumph of hedonism over restraint, but hedonism had to be of the approved sort. The downfall of Oscar Wilde in 1895 was a savage and effective reminder to even the most brilliant of writers that there were official lines to be drawn, beyond which lay social ruin and, in Wilde's case, financial ruin—he was destroyed as an artist and the collapse of his health led to his early death in the first year of the twentieth century.

It was ironic that this most modern of men should have survived the sentence of two years' hard labour—which was expected to break someone of his background and temperament—only to die in 1900, the beginning of a century whose delight in international celebrity he had anticipated in his meteoric rise and talent for self-promotion.

Wilde's last first night (*The Importance of Being Earnest*) had taken place at the St James's Theatre in King Street, St James's, near Christie's auction house and the gentlemen's clubs of St James's Street. Sixty years later Vivien Leigh was to lead a protest against its closure, a protest she took all the way to the House of Lords, but which failed to halt this most elegant building's destruction and replacement with an office block.

George Alexander, who played Jack Worthing in the original production of *The Importance of Being Earnest*, was manager of the St James's Theatre from 1891 to his death in 1919. In many ways he typified the breed of actor managers who dominated the first twenty years of the twentieth century, replacing the heavy repertory of nineteenth-century managers with dashing plays that showed off their good looks and ensured a large, regular, swooning army of female fans.

Born in 1858, Alexander was classically handsome in the same way as Haydn Coffin and William Terriss, though he escaped the fate of Terriss—the greatest matinee idol of his day—who had been stabbed, aged fifty, at the stage door of the Adelphi theatre, in Maiden Lane. The door was surmounted by a coat of arms, and can still be seen, slightly to the side of the current stage door. Just down the road from this spot is Rules, the theatre restaurant which still preserves, through its atmosphere, decor, many and old-fashioned tradition of service, the ambience of Victorian and Edwardian London.

William Terriss was physically slaughtered by a deranged actor, but George Edwardes was nearly driven mad by the antics of an actress—Mrs Patrick Campbell. Born Beatrice Stella Tanner, her mother's Italian blood was clearly in evidence in Stella's dark-haired beauty. Her husband, whose name she made famous, was killed in the Boer War, and in later years she grew increasingly difficult. Although her beauty diminished along with her friends—one of whom described her as being like a sinking battleship that resolutely opened fire on her would-be rescuers—she retained her wit. One such occasion involved her pet dog, whom she always carried with her (usually with disastrous consequences, including one time when she smashed her knee against a carriage step as she wouldn't drop the dog and use her hand to save herself after slipping on ice).

When her taxi, carrying her to the theatre, pulled up outside, the driver smelt, then saw, a puddle on the floor. "Who did that?" he snarled, looking at the dejected animal. "I did!" she bellowed, sweeping out of the cab and through the stage door.

She seemed to take a special delight in upsetting Alexander, and so determined was he never to act with her again, that when George Bernard Shaw offered him the opportunity to play Professor Higgins in *Pygmalion*, he refused to accept unless some actress other than Stella Campbell were to play Eliza. Shaw stuck to his guns as he was an enormous admirer of her (their correspondence, over many years, makes fascinating reading), and eventually the part went to the far less appropriate, though no less distinguished, Herbert Beerbohm Tree.

Sir Herbert Beerbohm Tree, the half-brother of the wit, theatre critic and writer Max Beerbohm, was another in the great fellowship of Edwardian actor managers, along with the likes of Frank Benson, Lewis Waller, Sir John Martin-Harvey, Harley Granville-Barker and Sir Johnston Forbes-Robertson.

All these men, along with a number of their contemporaries, were described in Hesketh Pearson's slim but fascinating book on actor managers, published in 1950. In it he says that the two most impressive male voices that he ever heard on stage belonged to Johnston Forbes-Robertson and Lewis Waller, the latter's being like a superb trumpet, ringing clear across the stage.

This is an apt description, not just of Waller's voice, but of his roles, full of heroic bravado and derring-do. The very titles of the plays he starred in conjure up the man and his manner: *Brigadier Gerard*, *A White Man*, *The Fires of Fate*, *The Duke's Motto*, *The Three Musketeers*, *Bardelys the Magnificent*, *The Harlequin King*.

Waller inspired devotion in his female fans to a degree not matched until the advent of Rock and Roll later in the century. Not content with queuing for hours to get the closest seats and best views of their hero, his fans wore large badges with the initials KOW. (Keen on Waller). Although pleased by such demonstrations of his popularity, Waller—like most of his rivals—was more interested in the box office takings than anything else, and when the news of Queen Victoria's death was announced by the paper boys who used to patrol most London streets selling the latest editions, he burst into tears—not with grief for a much-loved monarch but horror at the effect her demise would have on the box-office income!

Ticket sales provided the bottom line for every actor-manager, and they all tended to rely on one of (like Forbes-Robertson, who had both *Hamlet* and the Jerome K Jerome play *The Passing of the Third Floor Back* in his repertoire) two guaranteed favourites to cover any possible failures with new plays. One such standby was *The Scarlet Pimpernel* by Baroness Orczy.

This was originally written (with her husband) as a play, in 1903, and premiered in Nottingham. By 1905 it had reached London and had also been turned into a novel, not least to help market the play—a very early example of merchandising! With it the husband

and wife team of Fred Terry and Julia Neilsson had the greatest hit of their long and distinguished careers, and it kept them in clover for a further thirty years.

One reason for this was that audiences were happy to see their heroes—and heroines—despite their ages. Johnston Forbes-Robertson was a forty-year old Hamlet and was still performing the role in his sixties, while Sir John Martin-Hervey was playing the role of Sydney Carton aged seventy-six!

Carton had been the hero of Charles Dickens' *A Tale of Two Cities*, of course. Martin-Hervey, who had learned his trade under Sir Henry Irving at the Lyceum, adapted Dickens' story, retitling it *The Only Way*. Dickens would, I am sure, have approved. The great writer was in many ways a would-be actor. He greatly enjoyed amateur dramatics all his life, and his public readings from his works were like concert performances of plays.

Knowing the tastes of his audience (and the Victorian age, let us remember, was the golden age of melodrama) he chose the goriest, as well as the most dramatic, excerpts from his novels. The scene, from *Oliver Twist*, where Bill Sykes brutally murders Nancy, was a particular favourite, and so powerful was his performance that women used regularly to faint during his readings!

Martin-Hervey was an athletic performer, whereas Sir Johnston Forbes-Robertson was more of an aesthete—the John Gielgud of his day, famous for his delicate yet grand looks, his intelligence, and the beauty of his voice. Combining classic roles (Hamlet, Romeo) with new creations (Caesar in George Bernard Shaw's *Caesar and Cleopatra*), he played opposite Mrs Patrick Campbell, finding her far more congenial as a stage partner than poor George Alexander ever did. He also played in Shaw's *The Devil's Disciple*, though his relation with the playwright could be somewhat strained—as, to be fair, was most people's relationship with GBS.

By way of contrast, Sir Frank Benson was as gifted an athlete as he was an actor, and was famous (and frequently parodied) for choosing his casts for their sporting prowess as much as for their acting ability. Adverts for a Laertes who was a good spin-bowler may have been apocryphal, but they summed up his delight in friendly cricket matches against other theatres.

This athleticism was definitely a part of his stage technique, and a Benson show was guaranteed to make sword-fighting a prominent part of the production rather than a brief bit of background to the drama and poetry of the play. Given his taste for histrionics and the flash of cold steel under the theatre lights, it was entirely appropriate that it was after a performance of *Julius Caesar* (plenty of knives on show in the assassination scene), at the Theatre Royal, Drury Lane, that Benson received the touch of cold steel on his shoulder blades when King George V knighted him in the royal box.

George V (who reigned from 1910 to 1936) visited Drury Lane a number of times, one of them being in 1935, when Queen Mary, his wife, persuaded him to take her to see Ivor Novello's great musical, *Glamorous Night*. The King later met Novello, who was presented to him at a Buckingham Palace Garden Party. "Mr Novello, we greatly enjoyed the play, but in future please ensure that your plays have a happy ending. This one made the Queen cry. Try not to do so again!"

The royal box can still be seen at Drury Lane, where the Theatre Royal organises excellent backstage tours. One of the many points of interest is not just that there is a royal box but that, uniquely in London (and, indeed, British) theatre, there are two royal boxes—and two royal staircases.

These date from an unpleasant and unseemly scuffle between the two previous King Georges—George III and his son, the then George, Prince of Wales (later King George IV). Father and son hated each other, and when the King saw the Prince of Wales crossing the same lobby as him, he hurled himself on the appalled heir to the throne and had to be pulled off! After this the management of the theatre decided that such an event could not be permitted to happen again, so in addition to the Royal Box they created a Prince's Box, with a royal staircase to go with it, and to this day the two halves are referred to as the King's Side and the Prince's Side.

When Frank Benson was knighted by George V, he had been playing Shakespeare's Caesar, not Shaw's, but by the end of the decade Shaw was an established playwright. This was a great improvement on his nineteenth-century career, when he had been principally known as a critic. His twentieth-century career saw, in its first ten years, plays like *Captain Brassbound's Conversion*, *You Never Can Tell*, *Man and Superman* and *Mrs Warren's Profession*.

Captain Brassbound's Conversion co-starred Ellen Terry, Irving's ex-partner and a great beauty, as well as the most famous actress, of the nineteenth century. By now, she was past her prime (though she lived until 1928 and appeared in a silent film, *The Bohemian Girl*, with Ivor Novello, Gladys Cooper and Constance Collier). Her Bohemian lifestyle cost her the title that Irving had achieved, for although she was eventually made a Dame, she was only given the honour when an old woman, a few years before her death. In some ways, the unforgiving public morality of Victorian England lived on well into the following century.

As she got older, Ellen Terry found it increasingly hard to remember her lines, a fact that infuriated Shaw who was in the habit of berating even work-perfect actors, usually over some minor or imagined fault in pronunciation. This aggression led Ellen Terry to find it even harder to come out with her lines at a rehearsal of *Captain Brassbound*, so she stayed silent. Shaw lost his patience with this giant of the theatre and said furiously, "It doesn't matter what you say, dear lady—just say something!"

Shaw got his come-uppance on another occasion, when he sat in on a rehearsal of *Macbeth*, which was being taken by Harley Granville Barker. The young Jack Hawkins (1910–1973) who was later to become an international film star, records in his entertaining and informative autobiography (*Anything for a Quiet Life*, Elm Tree Books, 1973) that when Shaw interrupted and attacked the pronunciation of the work *Scone*, John Laurie, the Scottish actor who was to find a later television film as the dour Scottish undertaker in *Dad's Army*, angrily told Shaw that he had got the pronunciation wrong, and that he was not going to be told how to pronounce an old Scottish word by an Irishman! For once in his life, GBS realised when he was beaten and beat a hasty retreat!

Shaw's plays dealt with a wide variety of subjects, including, in *Mrs Warren's Profession*, the taboo one of prostitution. This was typical of Victorian public hypocrisy, in that London had tens of thousands of prostitutes, many of them under-aged. Places of public entertainment, such as theatres, were well-known pick-up places for the girls, and the promenade at the Empire, Leicester Square (since demolished and now a major cinema) was a notorious area for ladies of ill-repute.

One reason for their targeting of theatres was the fact that the audiences would mill about late at night on their way home, the development of fast and regular trains from central London to outer London and the suburbs having made late-night theatre-going possible for the middle and lower-middle classes, as well as for the wealthy who lived in fashionable, central areas like Mayfair, St James's and Belgravia.

The well-to-do could afford to spend more time at the numerous restaurants that catered for the after-theatre crowd, and in addition to obvious society venues like the Cafe Royal (which survived the scandal of having been the regular haunt of Oscar Wilde and his friends, but which never quite recaptured the style and splendour of the 1890s) there were numerous establishments in and around Regent Street and Piccadilly Circus, to cater for the clients of the theatres in the nearby Haymarket, St James's, and Shaftesbury Avenue.

If the 1900s saw a new breed of actor-manager and playwright, they also saw a golden age of theatre building and renovation. Most prominent among them was the London Coliseum, Oswald Stoll's great palace of a theatre, designed by Frank Matcham, and decked out like some vast monument from Imperial Rome, with classic symbols and heavy purple drapes on either side of the enormous proscenium arch.

With a stage area as large as the auditorium—which was itself the largest in London—the building lived up to its name. It employed the latest in modern technology, including a hydraulically operated curtain that relied on the Thames for its operation. Less successful was the mechanised Royal Box, a gimmicky contraption that, like all such things, failed to work. On the first visit of Edward VII (the Coliseum opened in 1904) the Royal box, which was precisely that, and was designed to carry the august personages from the front door all the way to the more conventional box from which they were to view the performance, got stuck on its specially constructed rails. The management were mortified, the Royal party was not amused (though perhaps the ghost of Queen Victoria might well have been), and the Royal Box was unceremoniously demoted to become part of the stalls foyer box office!

The Coliseum aimed to provide an all-round service for its clients, which is why almost as much attention was paid to the conservatory-style restaurant and the assorted bars, as to the auditorium and backstage areas. This attention to detail was a feature of other new theatres which, though smaller, nonetheless aimed for just as much opulence and sense of an elegant night out as did the Coliseum.

One such establishment was the Aldwych Theatre, next door to the Waldorf Hotel (built after the Aldwych Theatre had already opened), whose palm court is a model of Edwardian English civilisation, a reminder of a more elegant world. Built by Seymour Hicks and Charles Frohman (an American producer), the theatre was designed by W G R Sprague, who was also responsible for the Glove (now the Gielgud) and the Queen's Theatre in Shaftesbury Avenue.

Among others opened during this period were Wyndhams and the New, both owned (and built back to back) by Sir Charles Wyndham, an actor-manager who had served in the American Civil War (on the Union side!) and who was married to his beautiful leading lady, Mary Moore. Charles Wyndham opened the theatre that he had (modestly) named after himself in 1900, with a production of *Cyrano de Bergerac*, in which Wyndham played the lead.

One of the unexpected successes at Wyndhams in these first ten years of the century was a play called *An Englishman's Home*, by Guy du Maurier, son of George du Maurier, the novelist (who wrote *Trilby*, and created the character of Svengali) and brother of Gerald du Maurier, the great actor-manager whose management of the Wyndhams began in 1910.

An Englishman's Home was performed in 1909, and was an immediate hit because it tapped into a mood abroad in the nation—that of fear of a German invasion. The arms race, and in particular the naval race, with Germany had been going on for ten years, but perhaps the death of Queen Victoria added a further layer of insecurity to a nation that had received a severe shock during the Boer War—which had produced the popular music hall song, "Good-Bye Dolly Gray".

This was Guy's only theatrical success, whereas his brother, Gerald, was to become one of the great leading men in British stage history, a knight of the realm, a well-dressed inspiration to men and an object of admiration to his countless female fans. Du Maurier's sex appeal and steady success with women (despite having a wife and children, one of whom, Daphne, was to become a popular novelist, writer of *Rebecca* and of the play, *September Tide*) was not due to his looks, but to his manner.

Du Maurier represented, more even than past masters like George Alexander, the art of cool sophistication on stage, from his elegant yet un-showy clothes down to his slightest mannerism. Cigarettes were turned into a fashion accessory for and, appropriately, a brand of cigarettes was named after him. These are still available, I am told, but one has to go to Gibraltar to get them!

One of Du Maurier's most interesting roles was as Raffles (1906), at the Comedy Theatre. This play, based on the stories by E W Hornung, told the story of the public-school-educated gentleman thief, aided by his schoolfriend, nicknamed Bunny. Raffles in many ways typified the Edwardian approach to life—he may have been a burglar but he only picked on the very rich, he treated the whole things as a game, as a test of his wits against those of other gentlemen and the police. The police, needless to say, were represented as being of quite another class, and were always frustrated by Raffles' superior intellect. Such a "hero" would have been unthinkable on the mid-Victorian stage, but in the more relaxed atmosphere of Edwardian England he seemed an amusing, well-mannered joke.

Gerald du Maurier went on to play in another criminal play at the Comedy, called *Alias Jimmy Valentine* (1910), and it was not until the 1920s (see chapter on the 'twenties) that he turned to the other side of the law, playing a determined ex-officer, Bulldog Drummond, who, as his name implies, is determined to save England from internal and external threats—especially the Bolsheviks.

Du Maurier was preceded at the Comedy Theatre by Dame Marie Tempest, who had begun her career in operetta, but went onto to star in "straight" plays she performed at the Comedy– they were *Mrs Dot* and *Barbarity*, both written by Somerset Maugham, who at one point in this period had four plays running simultaneously in London.

This spectacular success was given the compliment of being satirised in *Punch* (then required reading for cultured members of the middle classes), which printed a cartoon showing a grumpy-looking ghost of William Shakespeare standing in front of a wall plastered with playbills advertising Maugham's current crop of plays.

Somerset Maugham is generally thought of, these days, in connection with the 1920s and 1930s, and with stories about British expatriate life in the Far East. He does indeed belong to that period and that area in particular, but he was a successful playwright long before the 'twenties, and was a product of the late Victorian era.

Among the leading actors of the early 1900s who appeared in his plays was Charles Hawtrey, in whose company the young Noel Coward was to learn so much—though his constant questions and precocious attitude sometimes tested Hawtrey's patience. Hawtrey produced Maugham's first play, *A Man of Honour*, and was later to star in *Home and Beauty*. Imitation is supposed to be the sincerest form of flattery, but one doubts if Charles Hawtrey would have been amused to learn that a young, camp, actor would take his name and become one of the leading (and outrageous) lights of the *Carry On* film series from the 1950s to the 1970s!

Looking back on the beginning of the century, one is astonished at the sheer vibrancy of the theatre scene. In addition to new theatres being built and opened, old ones like the Adelphi were being refurbished. The Adelphi, for example, was re-opened in the year of Victoria's death with the appropriate name of New Century—though the public preferred the old name, which was swiftly restored to it. The British, after all, are not over-fond of change in any sphere of activity.

The Adelphi featured Oscar Asche in *The Taming of the Shrew*, and a number of musicals such as *The Quaker Girl*, produced by George Edwardes, who was better known for running the Gaiety Theatre, where his showgirls were of legendary beauty. "Gaiety Girls" were all the rage in Edwardian London, and the shrewdest among them made sure that they married well. It was quite common for well-born young men to marry showgirls, who brought some much-needed new blood into old aristocratic families, rather like the American heiresses who were also welcomed with open arms (and empty wallets) by families who were prepared to swap titles for ready cash. Lily Langtry may have found herself a future king, but even chorus girls could hope to catch a count or land a lord.

The fluidity of the English class system has always been its strength, but so has the fact that although the rules are bent for beauty and new wealth, they are firmly enforced the rest of the time and towards anyone other than the occasional American cattle-baron's daughter or leading light of the West End stage.

The fact that those born to lower positions in life might actually be better equipped for management than their social "superiors" was rarely considered, and was not seriously challenged until after the carnage of the First World War, which makes James Barrie's play *The Admirable Crichton* (1902) all the more remarkable.

The Admirable Crichton tell of how an aristocratic family is shipwrecked and the butler, Crichton, takes charge. Once rescued and back in civilisation, however, the butler and the family act as if the whole episode hadn't happened, as if to acknowledge it would destroy the fabric of their individual lives, as well as offering a broader challenge to the general class system that underpinned the society of the time.

Middle- and upper-class audiences gained a pleasurable frisson from the play without feeling threatened—it was a comedy of manners, after all. The play did have a certain bite, though, and there was always far more to a Barrie play than was at first apparent.

His most successful one in this period, for example, was *Peter Pan*, first performed at the Duke of York's Theatre in December 1904, and which almost immediately achieved the classic status that it has retained ever since, fully justifying the author's confidence, despite the derision from some leading producers who should have known better. Gerald du Maurier created the role of Captain Hook, in which he was a terrifying spectacle—after all, he was supposed to be a frightening figure as much as a fun one.

The du Mauriers had a further connection with James Barrie, in that Gerald's sister was the wife of Arthur Llewellyn Davies, a young barrister, and mother of the boys befriended by Barrie after he had met them in Kensington Gardens, from and for whom the character of Peter Pan was born. In 1912, he arranged to have a sculpture of Peter Pan, by Sir George Frampton, erected in Kensington Gardens—a public gesture on the one hand, and a superb, and permanent, piece of advertising for his best-known play on the other.

The century began with Queen Victoria still on the throne, where she was to remain until her death in January 1901, and with many of the old certainties still in place, even though there was a sense of a new century and therefore a new beginning.

In many ways the century began some ten years earlier, with the Naughty Nineties, which seemed like a dress rehearsal for the gaiety and glamour of the reign of Edward VII (1901–1910). When the Queen passed away there was a great sense of sadness, of the end of an era, and the death of Sir Henry Irving, the first actor to be knighted, who passed away in 1905, seemed to reinforce the sense of change.

Indeed, it was almost as if he had made the gesture as the ultimate expression of loyalty to his queen, and as a recognition that the world in which he had shone as the leading Shakespearean and contemporary actor of his day had passed into history.

1900 saw the death of another archetypically Victorian figure, Oscar Wilde. Yet, in a paradox that was typical of the man and a feature of his wit and his work, he has been recognised by posterity as not only a symbol of the late Victorian world, and, in his trial, a victim of its uncompromising public morality, but as an extraordinarily modern man.

For Wilde was nothing if not a self-publicist, a celebrity in the modern sense who, a hundred years ahead of his time, used the modern media, particularly photography, to project an image of himself to his public, and to use his celebrity to boost the sales of his poems and books, and the takings at the box offices where his great comedies, particularly *The Importance of Being Earnest* (1895) were being performed.

This last play, his final first night, took place at the St James's Theatre in King Street, St James's, near Christy's auction house and the gentlemen's clubs of St James's Street. Sixty years later Vivien Leigh was to lead a protest at its closure, a protest she took all the way to the House of Lords, but which failed to halt this most elegant building's destruction and replacement with an office block.

Her protest was typical of the way in which actors of her generation had a great feeling for the history of their profession, and a love of the buildings in which they worked. Sadly, such an aesthetic interest, and a sense of continuity with the past, is fairly rare these days, although the formation, in 1996, of the Irving Society, gives some hope. Irving's statue stands at the end of the appropriately named Irving Street, at the side of the National Portrait Gallery (see chapter on the NPG).

Wilde was broken by the trial in 1895, and after his release from Reading Gaol, the subject of his famous poem, he lived in exile, in poverty, before dying in Paris in 1900—"This wall-paper is terrible. I cannot stand it. One of us will have to go." As soon as he had been found guilty his name was taken off the posters that advertised his plays, and it was not until some twenty years after his trial that his reputation as a dramatist began to recover from the notoriety of his private life.

George Alexander, who played Jack Worthing in the original production of *The Importance of Being Earnest*, like all his contemporaries, had a role that his public loved to see him in, and which would ensure a ready cash flow to make up for any disappointing box office receipts in more experimental productions. In his case, it was as *The Prisoner of Zenda* in Anthony Hope's swashbuckling Ruritanian adventure.

Lewis Waller's profile so excited his female fans that they formed a club, Keen on Waller, and wore large badges to his performances, with the initials of their club proudly displayed. These initials, KOW, led to unfortunate and unfriendly comments by ushers and members of the audience whose devotion to Mr Waller was rather calmer than their own!

Waller had hoped to be known as a "serious" actor, but Oscar Wilde had had the measure of the man. When asked about Waller's performance in *An Ideal Husband*, he merely replied that Waller would make an ideal d'Artagnan! In fact, his biggest success was in a period piece, *Monsieur Beauclaire*, that opened at the Comedy Theatre in 1902 and guaranteed his commercial future.

Fred Terry, similarly, had scored a huge hit in the title role of *The Scarlet Pimpernel* in 1905, a role he was to reprise over several decades. Sir John Martin-Harvey, another leading Edwardian actor-manager, had learned his trade under Henry Irving at the Lyceum, but adapted to the new tastes of the new century by adapting Charles Dickens' novel, *A Tale of Two Cities*. Retitled *The Only Way*, it was his most profitable show. He played Sydney Carton, of course, and so successful was his noble progress to the guillotine that he was still playing the role in his last stage appearance in 1939, aged seventy-six!

Sir Johnston Forbes-Robertson had a favourite role, but it was more in keeping with the classic roles expected of an actor-knight: Hamlet. He first played the role in 1897 aged fifty-four, and was to carry on as the doomed prince well past retirement age. He certainly would not have agreed with modern method acting, for he saw acting as a necessary task that he couldn't wait to finish, and claimed that he never once went on to the stage without wishing for that magic moment when the curtain finally falls on the last scene.

Julius Caesar had been the subject of one of the many plays by that other great Irish dramatist, George Bernard Shaw. His *Caesar and Cleopatra* (1906) came halfway in a series of plays that had begun with *Widower's Houses* in 1902, found favour with *The Devil's Disciple* (1897), touched on the forbidden subject of prostitution in *Mrs Warren's Profession* and had started the century with what has turned out, over the following hundred years, to be perhaps his most popular play, *You Never Can Tell* (1900). This first decade also saw *Captain Brassbound's Conversion* (1900), *Man and Superman* (1903), *Major Barbara* (1905) and *The Doctor's Dilemma* (1906).

The 1910s seemed to begin with a continuation of the 1900s, in that the same generation of actor-managers were producing plays and Mr Shaw was still writing them—*Misalliance* (1910), *Fanny's First Play* (1911), Androcles and the Lion (1913) and *Pygmalion* (1913).

Theatre feuds—those intense, savagely witty, mind-blowingly petty, wonderfully grand disputes between towering egos—were still in full flood, crossing the decades as easily as if thoroughbreds were leaping fences. The most thoroughbred of them all, Mrs Patrick Campbell, had driven George Alexander mad at the St James's Theatre, and he refused to act on the same stage with her.

When, therefore, George Bernard Shaw offered Alexander the plum role of Professor Higgins in *Pygmalion*, Alexander replied that he would be delighted to do so, provided that Mrs Patrick Campbell was not engaged to play Eliza. He would, he assured Shaw, pay any other actress any amount of money, so long as he didn't have to play opposite that hateful woman. She would drive him insane. Shaw stuck to his guns and the part of Professor Higgins had to go to Sir Herbert Tree instead.

Tree was another larger-than-life figure who loved showy parts, and whose most reliable play was *Trilby*, by George Du Maurier. He too had turned down a plum part, that of Captain Hook, in Sir James Barrie's *Peter Pan* (1904). When asked why he disliked the role he famously replied, with a witticism that also reflected the semi-divine status that the Edwardian actor-managers seemed to enjoy: "God knows, and I have promised to tell no one else."

Within a few years of its opening, *Peter Pan* was an acknowledged classic, and a glittering succession of England's leading ladies were to play Peter for the rest of the century. Among the earlier ones were Fay Compton and Gladys Cooper. Later Anna Neagle, best known as Queen Victoria and a number of plucky upper-class women in a variety of wars, was also to play Peter, with more than a touch of the scout mistress about her/him.

Barrie was in many ways a typically Edwardian playwright, despite being more innovative and intelligent than many of his contemporaries.

If *Peter Pan* was a whimsical fantasy that appealed to one aspect of his audience, his other plays addressed contemporary issues that were beginning to make themselves felt in a society that was rich and superficially, confident, but which was beginning to worry about possible disasters lying in wait.

What Every Woman Knows (1908) sympathises with the rising tide of feminism that was to find its most vocal outlet in the suffragette movement, while *The Admirable Crichton* (1902) had made a wry comment on the English class structure that was to suffer a severe though not yet fatal blow—it was to take twenty years and another World War to mortally wound it.

The disaster of the First World War was presaged in 1912 by the sinking of the *Titanic*, a disaster that seemed to warn the increasingly affluent and technologically advanced twentieth century that its civilisation was far more vulnerable to catastrophe than it liked to think.

As the arms race in Europe got faster and more threatening, and the Balkans exploded into a series of savage little conflicts, the theatre-going public in England turned to colour and music, to spectacular and exotic entertainment to take their minds off foreign problems, and off the domestic crises, such as Lloyd George's budget, reform of the House of Lords, dock strikes and Irish revolutionaries, that appeared like thunder clouds in the blue afternoon skies of the Edwardian summer.

Catching the popular mood, Oscar Asche, another impresario/actor who had worked with Benson and with Tree, put on *Kismet* in 1911 and *Chu Chin Chow* (1916) which became the biggest hit of the First World War.

There had been plays warning of the dangers of German invasion in the years prior to the War, but once the full horror of the Western Front was experienced, soldiers on leave, and their families, wanted light-hearted entertainment. They wanted to escape the war, not be reminded of it. This is why shows like *Chu Chin Chow* and a new form of revue, with shows like *Tabs* and *Who's Hooper?* were immensely popular. Both these revues featured music by the young Ivor Novello (1893–1951), who had come to popular attention through his poignant and moving song, "Keep the Home Fires Burning" in 1914.

The 1920s

After the war finally ended with the Armistice of 11th November 1918, the British people wanted to celebrate. The war and the appalling flu epidemic which followed it, killing more people than had died on the battle field, had destroyed many social conventions, and had, in particular, liberated women, who now enjoyed the vote as well as greater spending power.

The war years had seen the development of cinema, which spread rapidly through the 'twenties and was to become even more popular with the advent of talkies, in Al Jolson's *The Jazz Singer* (1927). However, they had also been a period when more people than ever had gone to the theatre, if only to be with their loved ones on leave from the Front, and the theatres benefited from this experience.

The cross-over between cinema and stage that we see today, with stage actors subsidising their theatre appearances by making films, was happening even in the 1920s, though the balance was more of an equal one in those days. Ivor Novello's acting career, as opposed to composing, began in 1921, and was launched and subsequently helped by the fact that throughout the 1920s he was Britain's biggest male movie star.

In some ways the theatre scene showed a remarkable continuity, with George Bernard Shaw—*Heartbreak House* (1920), *Back to Methuselah* (1922), *Saint Joan* (1923) and *The Apple Cart* (1929)—and James Barrie—*Mary Rose* (1920) and *Shall We Join The Ladies?* (1922)—

still writing, and stars like Mrs Patrick Campbell still appearing before their devoted audiences.

This was an age of new reputations too, with many of those who were to become household names for the rest of the century making their mark. Shaw's *St Joan*, for example, was a triumph for Sybil (later Dame Sybil) Thorndike, while the socialite and beauty Lady Diana Cooper had a huge success in Max Reinhardt's production of *The Miracle* at the Lyceum.

Laurence Olivier, John Gielgud and Donald Wolfit, all to be actor knights in due course, began their careers in this decade and the Old Vic under Lilian Baylis (see separate chapter on the Old Vic) was to be a forcing ground for a galaxy of British stars. One of the greatest men of the theatre—hence his nickname of Master—was Noel Coward, whose years of apprenticeship as a child actor were now firmly behind him as he made his name first in revue—*London Calling* (1923)—and then with a devastating first play, *The Vortex*.

The Vortex dealt, variously, with drug taking, toy-boys and incest, and was an immediate sensation. The following year Coward produced one of his most enduring comedies, *Hay Fever*, in which he parodied the theatrical grand dames that he had grown up with, as well as the country house lifestyle to which, as a young man, he aspired.

Among the many trademarks that Coward adopted were the elegant way he held his cigarette. This was not as original as we think, for the most debonair of actors, Sir Gerald du Maurier, father of Daphne, the writer, not only carried a cigarette with the elegant ease with which he wore his immaculate clothes, he also had a brand of cigarettes (still available in Gibraltar) named after him.

Sir Gerald had starred in *The Admirable Crichton* in 1902, and in *Peter Pan* in 1904, but one of his best roles was as Raffles, the gentleman burglar who took the English obsession with the intelligent but determinedly amateur to its extreme. Du Maurier is considered the first leading man to have worn, as a matter of course, the same elegant clothes on stage as off, playing gentlemen in contemporary roles.

Supporters of George Alexander might have disagreed with this, but it is true that no one has ever quite come up to Du Maurier's reputation for effortless style. Perhaps the nearest equivalent in our own times was Rex Harrison. Like Harrison, Du Maurier was a ladies' man, a role in which he was notably successful, despite his lack of conventional good looks.

Not content with simply acting, Du Maurier moved into management at Wyndhams Theatre, where he was involved in putting on Edgar Wallace's plays. Wallace, a fascinating man who rose from dockland poverty to be Britain's most prolific crime novelist and journalist, was, for a period, almost as prolific on stage as he had been on page, but he made the mistake of wanting to produce plays as well as write them.

The Roaring 'Twenties passed in a blaze of publicity, terminating with the infamous stock market crash of 1929. This seemed an ill omen for the new decade, which after the election of Hitler as German Chancellor in 1933 seemed doomed to end in war.

The theatre of the 1930s continued to have its light side—after all, Terence Rattigan's first success, *French without Tears* (1936), was a comedy, and J B Priestley, another writer who achieved fame in this decade, produced the hilarious *When We Are Married* in 1938. However Priestley also wrote on more serious themes, as in *Time and the Conways* (1937) and the general mood was one of worry.

It was for this reason the Ivor Novello's musicals were so popular; although they related to contemporary events—*The Dancing Years* (1939) was a direct response to Nazi Germany's Anschluss with Austria in 1938—they were, in the main, escapist fantasies that owed more to Edwardian operetta than to jazz-age musicals or the world of inter-war economic depression.

Noel Coward caught this need for escapism too. *Cavalcade* (1931) had been a tear-inducing evening of nostalgia at Drury Lane. *Private Lives* (1930), perhaps his most popular play, enabled the middle classes to forget their falling share prices by looking and laughing at the world of the idle rich. *Design For Living* (1933) was a similar peek into a privileged world, although it seemed to belong more to the early 'twenties than the 'thirties.

The original production of *Private Lives*, in which Coward played opposite the incomparable Gertrude Lawrence (1898–1952), also starred the young Laurence Olivier. Although he possessed enormous talent, he was still young and self-indulgent enough to have fits of the giggles on stage. Coward was determined to cure him of this, and did so, though it took a considerable amount of time and effort on both their parts.

Olivier was, in a very twentieth century way, to become known for his private life as much as for his professional one, and indeed the two overlapped to a remarkable degree, thanks to his romance with and marriage to Vivien Leigh.

Born in Darjeeling in 1913, on Fireworks Night, appropriately enough, to wealthy English parents, Vivien came to England to be educated at a convent school, before going to Europe to be "finished". This was not so much a session at a "finishing school" like other girls, as a series of cultural visits throughout Europe, that made her a remarkable well-travelled and cultured woman.

She found it easy to marry a suitable attractive and wealthy barrister, having seen off his fiancée in a manner worthy of Scarlet O'Hara, whom she was to play in *Gone With The Wind* in 1939. Despite her marriage and a young daughter, she was determined to be an actress, and won critical acclaim in *The Mask of Virtue* (1935) and *The Happy Hypocrite* (1936).

Her other ambition, on seeing him in action, was to capture Olivier's heart which, despite his marriage to the actress, Jill Esmond, and a baby son (Tarquin) she did. The theatre world realised the extent of their relationship when Vivien played Ophelia to Olivier's Hamlet at Elsinore in Denmark in 1937. For the next twenty-plus years they were to be best-known and glamorous couple in show-business.

While Olivier was earning a reputation as a Shakespearean actor, and as a lover, Ralph Richardson was making a name for himself at the Old Vic and in the West End, while John Gielgud, scion of the Terry acting dynasty, had carved a name for himself as the greatest Shakespearean actor of his day, specialising in Hamlet and Richard II, also playing the latter in *Richard of Bordeaux*.

Gielgud's well-deserved reputation of kindliness and generosity was demonstrated in his help towards the young Alec Guinness who had literally to walk across London in order to meet his idol, who gave him advice and ten pounds (worth a great deal more in the 1930s), and who was later to be one of the many admirer's of Guinness's performance as Hamlet, a role that Gielgud had, more than any other actor since Sir Johnston Forbes-Robertson, made his own. Whatever the trends or characteristics of the acting world in the 1920s and 1930s, they were, as we know now, doomed decades, and the stage was to be as radically damaged and changed by the Second World War as the rest of society.

The 1940s

This decade was, of course, dominated by the war, which had a far greater effect on London's theatreland than the First World War had. The constant threat of German bombing raids, particularly from 1939 to 1941, and then in the last stages of the war, from V1 and V2 rockets, meant that theatre-going was a somewhat hazardous business.

Putting on shows was all the more difficult, of course; partly the problems in touring shows under wartime conditions, partly the fact that many of the younger and more experienced actors were called up for service in the armed forces.

The career of Sir Donald Wolfit, one of the last of the great actor-managers until the advent of Kenneth Branagh, is all the more remarkable given these hurdles. In a remarkably involving and atmospheric play (and subsequent film), *The Dresser*, Ronald Harwood, who acted under and was dresser to Sir Donald, shows both the bonhomie and the bitchiness of theatre life, together with the indomitable spirit of "Sir", who performs several different lead Shakespeare roles a week.

Wolfit's determination to keep the theatrical flag flying, both in London, with scenes from Shakespeare at the Strand Theatre, and on tour in big provincial cities like Liverpool, whose docks were a prime target for bombers, were one of the more inspiring features of British theatre in the 1940s.

Many entertainers performed for ENSA (the armed forces entertainment service that was affectionately, and sometimes accurately known to the troops as Every Night Something Awful). Among them were Novello, who had been unjustly imprisoned on petrol rationing offences in 1944, and Noel Coward. Coward was a great friend of Lord Louis Mountbatten, who ended the war as Supreme Commander, South East Asia.

Coward gave morale-boosting performances throughout Asia, often at risk to his health. Nearer to home, his experience of the London blitz, and his admiration for the capital's inhabitants, produced one of his most evocative songs, "London Pride".

After the war there was a huge political change, with the landslide election of a Labour government under Clement Attlee, which was in itself indicative of a profound desire for social change. This was to find expression in the theatre as well as the ballot booth, but it was to take some ten years before it was expressed in so radical a way as to change the London stage forever.

In the meantime Olivier had finished the war with a stirring patriotic film, *Henry V*, under his belt. With one film he had vaulted over all the work that Gielgud had put into his stage career, to become in the public's eyes the greatest Shakespearean actor in England. He was determined to keep up the pressure on film—*Hamlet* (1948) and *Richard III* (1953)—but also, to be fair, wanted to prove himself on stage with the Old Vic theatre company at the New Theatre in St Martin's Lane, now called the Albery Theatre.

The 1940s had been a good decade for H M Tennent, the theatre management that under Hugh (Binkie) Beaumont came to dominate the West End for twenty years; then Beaumont's word was law in theatrical circles. Any actor or actress who was foolish enough to cross him would find it impossible to find work anywhere other than in the provinces.

This was unfair, and had its obvious disadvantages, but on the other hand Beaumont's taste was an educated and successful one until he began to lose his grip in the late 1960s, and he ensured that Shaftesbury Avenue, known simply as "the Avenue" in the trade, was constantly filled with well-made, well-dressed plays, and that the billboards outside the theatres were full of reliable star names that the public knew, and whom they flocked to see.

For despite the Blitz and the remaining bomb damage, theatre-going was still a fairly frequent event, and although much of the glamour of the 1920s and 1930s had been swept away, people still dressed for the theatre, and expected stars to act as stars offstage as well as behind the proscenium arch. This relatively cosy world was constantly challenged by the cinema, as it had been for thirty years, but in the 1950s it was unceremoniously shattered.

The 1950s

The theatre of the early to mid-1950s was in many ways a continuation of that of the 1940s. Terence Rattigan, who had risen to early fame with *French Without Tears* in 1936 and had written the war-time drama *Flare Path* in 1942, based on his own experiences in the RAF, had continued his exploration of the deeply repressed emotional life of the English middle classes with *The Winslow Boy* (1946) and *The Browning Version* (1948).

Rattigan, the Old Harrovian son of a diplomat, epitomised, in both his work and lifestyle, the elegance and stiff upper lip approach of the class from which he came. He personified the abstract image of a typical member of his audience as "Aunt Edna", middle-aged and middle class.

Much of the emotional power of his plays comes from the convention of decency, duty and restraint—especially in sexual matter, the central theme of *The Deep Blue Sea* (1952)—that typified Middle England at the time. Even though this was now a post-war world, the middle classes had not forgotten the shock of Edward VIII's abdication in 1936.

More to the point, perhaps, was that Rattigan and his circle had not forgotten the shock of the trial of Oscar Wilde, some sixty years earlier. Rattigan was a homosexual, at a time when the physical expression of his emotions was illegal and a disgrace. Many of the most powerful dilemmas of thwarted or repressed love and sexual desire that feature in his plays were based on the experiences of himself and his friends, but he had to turn them into heterosexual situations in order to make them acceptable to the general public and, until 1968, to the Lord Chamberlain.

In 1954, he wrote one of his best plays, *Separate Tables*. Like the earlier Browning version (which was one half of an evening, being followed after the interval by *Harlequinade*) it was a double bill, though on this occasion many of the same characters appear in both plays, which are set in a genteel hotel which is host to a variety of people who have been damaged by life.

This collection of characters is in many ways a symbol for a nation that had seen its glories and its future slip away, and was simply marking time in reduced circumstances. But beyond any allegorical content lies Rattigan's unrivalled ability to show us a section of English Society that is very much of its time, and is thus something of an exercise in social archaeology for the younger members of today's audiences.

Terence Rattigan was in many ways the pre-eminent exponent of the "well-made play", and it was his misfortune to still be at the height of his powers—as *Separate Tables* showed—when John Osborne launched his revolution at the Royal Court Theatre in 1956, with the appropriately named *Look Back in Anger*.

The Royal Court, under the auspices of the English Stage Company, was set in the East End of Sloane Square, the distinguished spot where the three wealthy, but distinct, areas of Chelsea, Knightsbridge and Belgravia all meet. Hardly the scene for a revolution, one might think, but *Look Back in Anger*, however conservative it seems today, was the first of the "kitchen sink" dramas, set a whole new tone and trend in British Theatre and rendered the elegant and well-dressed dramas that Rattigan specialised in redundant almost overnight.

Other notable victims of the dramatic change in critical taste was Christopher Fry, whose verse dramas, like *The Lady's Not For Burning* (1948), *A Sleep of Prisoners* (1951) and *The Dark is Light Enough* (1954), were rendered obsolete by John Osborne.

Born in 1929, John Osborne made his name as an "Angry Young Man", a reference to the title of his first and most famous play, and to the bile expressed by its lead character, Jimmy Porter. It is all the more ironic that by the end of his life (1994) he had metamorphosed into an Angry Old Man, lashing out at modern playwrights and trendy young directors, at the collapse of good manners and theatrical traditions, and at the very theatre, the Royal Court, where he had made his fortune.

All this was far in the future during the 1950s however, and the wunderkind of post-war British theatre followed up his 1956 success with a play the following year, *The Entertainer*. In a pairing that worked wonders for both men's careers—Osborne at the start of his, Olivier in a mid-life artistic crisis—Laurence Olivier, the epitome of glamorous West End theatre, took the plunge and played a seedy variety artiste in a play that was ostensibly about a fading performer but was just as much a metaphor for the post-Suez decline of Great Britain.

Not all plays were about Angry Young men, but from the mid-fifties they tended to be about a different class of man, and woman, than they had been before. Previously, the working class tended to appear as amiable fools, loyal servants or threateningly criminal. Now they were increasingly able to tell their own story.

Joan Littlewood's Theatre Workshop was at the forefront of this movement, producing Brendan Behan's *The Quare Fellow*, while outside London the Belgrade Theatre, Coventry, was a showcase for plays by new young writers like Arnold Wesker and Harold Pinter. Both men were to be leading lights of the 'sixties' stage, but had already made an impact in the 1950s, Wesker with *Chicken Soup With Barley* (1958), *Roots* (1959) and *The Kitchen* (1959); Pinter with *The Birthday Party* (1958) and *The Dumb Waiter* (1959).

While these new talents were bringing the realities of working class life to the attention of patrons in the stalls, the classics were still being performed at Stratford, and by the Old Vic Company. Actresses with old-world glamour like Vivien Leigh and Margaret Leighton were appearing regularly, even if Vivien Leigh's mental health often gave cause for concern, especially when under the stresses of touring productions.

Her fragility was not helped by the constant attacks of Kenneth Tynan, the theatre critic who worshipped her husband, Laurence Olivier, while seeming to take great pleasure in wounding Leigh whenever the opportunity arose. She was not helped either by the roles she was asked to play, and one of her greatest successes, as Blanche du Bois in *A Streetcar Named Desire*—which she first played in 1949—tipped her into a mental breakdown, such was the nature of her role and her identification with the character that she was playing.

It was largely because of her mood swings and manic-depression the Laurence Olivier found her impossible to live with, and there could have been nothing more symbolic of the change from the 1950s to the 1960s, in terms of the English stage, than the end of the Oliviers' marriage.

This revolutionary decade, that saw such enormous social, sexual and political upheaval and change, was strongly reflected and partly shaped, in Britain, at least, in the theatre.

The 1950s had in many ways been a turning back to the past, a doomed attempt to recreate the pre-war world of the 1930s, with the advantage of labour-saving devices in the home. The Labour government that had swept to power in 1945 was unceremoniously removed from office in 1951, and remained in opposition throughout the rest of the decade.

The fact that the Oliviers, now Sir Laurence and Lady Olivier, were still the most powerful and glamorous couple in theatre and film on both sides of the Atlantic throughout the 'fifties, as they had been in the late 'thirties and all through the 'forties, gave a sense of continuity, of permanence, to the theatre world. They seemed an expression of the wider conservatism of society at large.

Then the golden couple separated, and Olivier married a rising young actress of relatively humble origins, Joan Plowright, the occasion had a far more potent symbolism than the mere fact of a private divorce and marriage might warrant.

Here was the leader of the theatrical world rejecting the past and, literally embracing the present. In many ways, it set the scene for the floodgates that the 'sixties opened. Olivier's new lease of life was both personal—he was to have the longed-for family with Plowright that he had never achieved with Leigh—and artistic.

The 1960s saw him succeed at the new Chichester Theatre, then take up the reins as artistic director of the National Theatre, in which context he not only set up one of the two great theatre companies of the decade—the other being the Royal Shakespeare Company, which was created by Peter Hall—but pressed for a permanent home in which to house it. Filmed in *The Entertainer*, Olivier continued to play Shakespearean roles as well as new ones, and was a notable Othello in 1964 to Maggie Smith's Desdemona.

Joan Littlewood's Theatre Workshop continued to make the headlines, in particular with their extraordinarily powerful play, *Oh What Lovely War!* This scathing attack on the First World War was taken up by a generation who had grown up in the blitz and who were to protest with increasing determination as the decade progressed against the American involvement in the Vietnam War. The play was filmed by Richard Attenborough in 1969, at the height of the conflict.

The 'sixties saw many new talents flourish, but none was more typical of the decade, or more cruelly denied the chance to flourish beyond it, than that of Joe Orton. An ex-drama student who had lived for years in a bedsit with his more educated lover, Kenneth Halliwell, Orton had originally tried to make a career as a novelist, writing with Halliwell while both subsisted on a cheap diet of canned rice and jam, as far as one could get from Terence Rattigan in his elegant Belgravia apartment.

Titles like *The Boy Hairdresser* were typical of their attempted output, which got nowhere. It was only when Orton and Halliwell had each been jailed, separately, for six months for defacing books from Islington Library, which now proudly displays them to visiting scholars, that Orton was able to develop the confidence and flair to write on his own.

He was soon discovered as an original, if highly sexual and subversive playwright, whose unique blending of outrageous situations with straight-faced, epigrammatic, Wildean dialogue, produced a run of modern comic classics: *Entertaining Mr Sloane* (1969), *Loot* (1966) and *What the Butler Saw* (1969). The last of these, his best, was produced posthumously, as Halliwell, jealous of Orton's fame and fearful that Orton would leave him, murdered Joe Orton in 1967, as he was preparing to make a film with the Beatles, another typically 1960s' phenomenon.

Of the many other playwrights who flourished in this decade, and helped create the London of the Swinging 'Sixties, along with pop groups, models, hairdressers and clothes designers, the best known and longest lasting was Harold Pinter.

A master at showing the darker side of urban and family life, he became known for his trademark pauses, the gaps in conversation that reveal the gulf between individuals, yet are themselves so individual as to represent everything from monetary embarrassment or confusion to a menacing silence. Appropriately enough his last play of the decade was *Silence* (1969), but his pauses had appeared regularly in earlier plays like *The Caretaker* (1960) and *The Homecoming* (1965).

In his early plays, he drew on his own background as a Jewish boy in 1930s London, and he was excellent at creating a sense of suburbia that, far from being cosy and safe, contained distinct menace. It was in the 'sixties, and through his pauses, that the term "Pinteresque" was coined.

If Pinter was an avant garde but in some ways conservative playwright, *Beyond the Fringe* was a radically 'sixties' entertainment, satire, that sprang from the Oxbridge establishment yet bit the hand that fed, or at least educated, it.

Although not a part of mainstream theatre, the revue contained two later artistic figures of note, Alan Bennett and Jonathan Miller, a talented pianist/actor (Dudley Moore) and a brilliant wit (Peter Cook). If their satire was a distinctly 'sixties' phenomenon, the revue format had a long history, and in many ways their show drew as much from the 'fifties' traditions of shows like *Share My Lettuce* (Maggie Smith and Kenneth Williams, 1957) and the revues of Flanders and Swann.

Among a great many new talents who seemed to find their feet in this decade were Alan Ayckbourn (the most frequently performed British playwright after Shakespeare) and Tom Stoppard, the former a brilliant comedian who ruthlessly but hilariously dissected human nature through the medium of the middle classes, the latter a Czech-born writer whose works display enormous intelligence and an educated wit.

Undoubtedly the most momentous development in British theatre during the 1960s was the abolition of the Lord Chamberlain's right to censor plays. The Lord Chamberlain is the head of the Royal Household, one of the closest advisors of the Queen. The appointment of the Lord Chamberlain as guardian of the public morals had begun in the early eighteenth century, as a response to scurrilous attacks on the then government by radical playwrights. Originally a political gesture, it soon became a merely moral one, which was the source of great frustration to a great many writers through the years. The presence of the Lord Chamberlain's representative in the stalls, sitting with a copy of the approved script—all playscripts had to be sent to the Lord Chamberlain for approval before a licence to perform would be given—to check that the words on page and stage were the same, was a regular sight in English theatre for two and a half centuries.

The long overdue (indeed it was a disgrace that it had ever been allowed) reform led, in the short term, to the staging of sexually explicit shows like *Hair* (1968) and *Oh, Calcutta!* (1969), but in the long term, after this burst of adolescent, and very 'sixties, exuberance, it simply meant that challenging and controversial plays could be put on without any consideration other than box-office returns.

At the Royal Shakespeare Company, Trevor Nunn, who was to be a highly successful director over the remaining years of the century, took over from Peter Hall, who was, in turn, to take over the running of the National Theatre from Sir Laurence Olivier.

The 1970s

The new decade began with what seemed to be the apogee of Laurence Olivier's career, when he was made Britain's first theatre peer, albeit a "life" peer rather than a hereditary one. The gesture seemed not only to offer the arts another voice in the House of Lords, but to confirm his position as Britain's most influential actor—some of Sir John Gielgud's fans would certainly debate the point.

Just as Sir Henry Irving's position as Britain's first ever actor knight suggested that he was the pre-eminent actor of the nineteenth century, so Olivier's ennoblement appeared to suggest that the twentieth century belonged to him. In fact, the 1970s were to see Olivier suffer a succession of illnesses, and ill-health would plague him for the rest of his life.

He managed, against the odds, to rally in the face of physical illness, unlike his late wife (Vivien Leigh had died of tuberculosis in 1967) who had failed with her mental problems. The real blow that he suffered, however, was professional, when Peter Hall was appointed Director of the National Theatre in his place, on grounds of ill-health, and it was Hall, not Olivier, who took the National into its new home on the South Bank, a theatrical haven in a sea of windswept concrete wilderness.

Denys Lasdun's design may not have been everyone's idea of a theatre from the outside, but inside its three auditoria, one of them (in the round like a Greek or Roman theatre) named after Lord Olivier, and the spacious foyer with its live music, made and make an attractive, warm and welcoming venue.

Whether or not one entirely agrees with this view, the National was at least a new theatre. By the mid-1970s, when it opened, all too many provincial theatres had gone the way of England's country houses, and had been demolished or changed into other uses. Even the St James's Theatre, home of Oscar Wilde's greatest success, showcase for George Alexander's elegant Edwardian productions, had been demolished to make way for an office block, despite a massive campaign led by Vivien Leigh.

The first production at the National, in 1976, was of *Hamlet*, starring Albert Finney. A classic showpiece for every ambitious young actor, though Finney was not in the first flush of youth, this was a deliberate reference to the fact that Olivier had invited the young Peter O'Toole, fresh from his success in David Lean's film of *Laurence of Arabia*, to play the role in the first National Theatre production back in 1963.

O'Toole had made more of a name for himself as a film actor than on stage, though he was to return to Shakespeare, in a memorably disastrous *Macbeth*, in the 1980s.

The 1970s saw Peter Brook's ground-breaking production of *A Midsummer Night's Dream*, the creation of the Young Vic, the development of the London Fringe Theatre scene. This movement, born largely from Dan Crawford's pioneering work in a room at the back of a pub, the King's Head in Islington, spread throughout London, leading to minute theatres opening, and sometimes flourishing, in the most unlikely venues and the most unfashionable areas.

Although nothing could replace the collapse of the traditional rep theatre, the Fringe provided a London-based alternative theatre scene where albeit for little or no wage actors could learn their craft, meet each other, swap ideas, and experiment with new plays, in the way that theatre clubs had done in the dark days of the Lord Chamberlain's iron rule over what was or was not suitable for the general public.

The Lord Chamberlain, for example, would never have approved *The Rocky Horror Show*, which moved from the Royal Court Theatre to the King's Road and then to the West End, and was turned into a cult film along the way.

He wouldn't allow representations of stage of biblical characters either, so Andrew Lloyd Webber and Tim Rice's *Jesus Christ, Superstar* would not have become the huge success that it was—following on from another biblically-based musical, *Joseph and his Amazing Technicolour Dreamcoat*. The titles of these pieces are as period as their music, but both were to contribute to the extraordinary success both men were to enjoy in the 1980s. A further taste was however given with the success of the very 'seventies' musical *Evita*.

Inspired by a programme Tim Rice heard on a car radio, it made a heroine out of the wife of a quasi-fascist South American dictator. From such uninspiring-sounding material came a musical that not only challenged a dearth of good British musicals since the heyday of Lionel Bart, but heralded the comeback of the musical as a genre that would come to dominate the West End and Broadway to an unprecedented degree in the next decade.

While this theatre team was making artistic and financial progress, the 1970s saw Terence Rattigan's decline and death. His penultimate play, *Bequest to the Nation* (1970) had been on a historical theme, as had his play *Ross* (1960—on Laurence of Arabia). *Bequest to the Nation* dealt with Nelson and Lady Hamilton, she being the bequest of the title.

In this, she had been like that other famous mistress of British history, Nell Gwynn. Nelson hoped a grateful nation would protect Lady Hamilton: King Charles II famously asked on his deathbed, "Let not poor Nelly starve," but that's exactly what Nell Gwynn did, while Lady Hamilton met an ignominious end in disgrace and exile in Calais.

Rattigan's treatment by the British public was almost as cruel, for his post-1956 reputation lay in tatters, and he was reviled by the fashionable critics and commentators as an emotionally repressed chronicler of the lives of a discredited and unsympathetic ruling class. It took The King's Head, the pub theatre already referred to, to begin the long haul back to critical and popular acclaim with a performance of *The Browning Version* shortly before Rattigan died, in 1977. He was not to know the extent, particularly in the 1990s, to which he would be rehabilitated, but he did at least have the pleasure of seeing one of his most poignant and beautifully written pieces enthusiastically performed on a small London stage.

One cannot think well, love well, sleep well, if one has not dined well.
Virginia Woolf

At a dinner one should eat wisely but not too well, and talk well, but not too wisely.
Somerset Maugham

A good cook is like a sorcerer who dispenses happiness.
Elsa Schiaparelli

Only dull people are brilliant at breakfast.
Oscar Wilde, *An Ideal Husband*

Those who do not enjoy eating seldom have much capacity for enjoyment of any sort.
Charles William Elliot, *A Happy Life*

EPILOGUE

When I first arrived in London as a drama student I could not afford to visit any of the restaurants mentioned in this book but I studied and admired all the authors and actors who could do. The Australians who had arrived before me were Joan Sutherland, Germaine Greer, Clive James but the inspiration came from the dancer, Robert Helpmann who had come over much earlier and partnered Dame Margot Fonteyn in the Royal Ballet Company.

Helpmann was the one Australian who would have brought over recipes which are now famous and are often featured in the restaurants in this book. Among them was the dessert "Pavlova". In Australia there are many versions of it which every good mother teaches her daughters when they are knee-high. Also Helpmann, being born on a sheep farm in 1907 would have eaten lamb served a dozen different ways, from the roast with mint sauce on Sundays to a stew, a casserole, minced for Shepherd's Pie with onions, seasoned and served cold, or in a hot curry.

The "Pavlova" dessert originated in Australia:

6 egg whites	1¾ cups granulated sugar
1 tbsp corn starch	1 tsp distilled white vinegar
1¾ cups of heavy cream (whipped)	3 to 4 tbsps sugar
1 tsp vanilla extract	

Whisk egg whites until stiff. Sprinkle in 5 to 6 tbsps of sugar until eggs make a light stiff meringue. Sift the cornstarch and remaining sugar with egg whites and add the vinegar. Fold the mixture together to form stiff peaks and turn on to greased baking sheet. Preheat oven to 220° F. Reduce heat to 175° F after 30 minutes. Cook for 2—2½ hours. Cool completely. Whip cream (which should be at room temperature), add the sugar as the cream is thickening and the vanilla essence. Remove top of meringue shell and pour in whipped cream and fruit. Passion fruit, kiwi fruit are the traditional fillings, and garnish on top. Alternatively, leave cream in middle and fruit on top.

Helpmann's story reads like magic. His mother was an actress but gave it up after she married. His father was a farmer and was strongly opposed when his son wanted to go into the theatre, however his mother prevailed and he began dance classes.

A few years later on advice of a friend who had seen him dance, his mother took him to see a dancer in Melbourne for lessons.

The dancer was Anna Pavlova.

She immediately recognised his talent and wanted him to return with her to Europe.

His father refused, and Robert was not allowed to go. Several years later, after working for J C Williamson in musical comedies, a British actress who was touring in Australia, Margaret Rawlings, persuaded his parents to allow him to go back to England with her and her husband.

Thus began his illustrious career. He quickly became famous, and during the 'forties and 'fifties reached the pinnacle of his career by partnering Dame Margot Fonteyn in the Royal Ballet Company at the Royal Opera House, and their work together has become legendary. He was not only their lead dancer but choreographed new ballets as well. When his film career took off he became an international star. Films such as *The Red Shoes* and *The Tales of Hoffmann* showed his dancing and choreography to the world. His face was extraordinary, and he made the most of it by playing exotic characters with extraordinary make-up highlighting his large eyes and bizarre costumes. He had a unique talent, and leading theatrical figures recognised his genius. Working together with Sir Frederick Ashton, they were the leading dancers and choreographers for the Royal Ballet.

Michael Benthall was an established theatre director, part of the British establishment, and he and Robert lived together in an elegant Eaton Place apartment where they entertained the creme de la creme of the theatre world. He was fascinated by Vivien Leigh and became her close friend and companion, especially when she was splitting up with Laurence Olivier.

When Michael Benthall became the Artistic Director of the Old Vic Company in the early 'fifties, Helpmann began his acting career. His life as a ballet star was slowly becoming that of a straight actor. He worked on his voice, and played his first Hamlet for Tyrone Guthrie. When Nureyev defected from Russia and began dancing with Fonteyn, Robert moved on to become a classical actor, something that no one else had achieved. When Benthall asked Katharine Hepburn to play the lead in Shaw's *The Millionairess* he opened it on Broadway with Robert playing the male lead, then took it to London. Helpmann and Hepburn became a team, and it was a mutual admiration society.

Then in 1955 Benthall organised a tour of Australia for the Old Vic Company with the two of them playing the leads in *The Merchant of Venice*, *The Taming of the Shrew* and *Measure for Measure*. Helpmann played Shylock, Petrucchio and Angelo.

Hepburn played Portia, Katharine and Isabella.

I was fortunate enough to be included in the company, and for six months we toured the capital cities of Australia. It was the first time Helpmann had returned to Australia for twenty-five years, so the press was out in full force, especially as he was accompanied by Katharine Hepburn. I remember we had a party for the company on arrival in Sydney, and Kate announced she would be hiring a bicycle to get around Sydney, so would not be using the car supplied (these were the days before stretch limousines).

The two were seen everywhere together, there was even talk of an intimate relationship but Kate was in the midst of her affair with Spencer Tracey at that time, so it seemed unlikely. After the show every night, she would put through a long-distance call to Los Angeles, and she would often be late for some after-show event, by a longer conversation than usual with Spencer. The Mayor of Sydney held a reception for the company, and we were all given the "keys of the city" at a lavish party, when Kate gave a short speech about how much she loved coming to Australia and how she was looking forward to seeing as much of the country as possible.

When we arrived in Brisbane we once again had a large reception, with Kate and Robert being photographed for all the newspapers. Australians flocked to see her, and the theatre was sold out. During our third week in Brisbane, it was announced that we would have the fifth week—our last week—off! Kate wanted to see the Great Barrier Reef so much, we were told, that she had bought out the theatre for the entire week's run, so she could spend the week on the Reef.

Surfer's Paradise, a resort on the coast just outside Brisbane, has a lovely beach, and in those days had private homes on the dunes and was relatively deserted. Today it resembles Miami Beach with high-rise hotels, shopping malls and masses of tourists. Gillian Anstey, one of the other actresses in the company, had become my closest friend, and when I was offered a large beach house at Surfer's Paradise by an old friend, Peter Huyber's mother, we readily accepted it for the week.

I can still remember the salty air and the sandy front steps as we unlocked the front door and heard the surf pounding outside. It was sheer heaven, and we'd sit at the front window looking out on the beach and the pounding waves lulled us to sleep every night. The contrast between our life in London was immense. We were euphoric. Sitting in the surf in the baking hot sun looking at the powdery white sand stretching for miles was a challenge to be reckoned with when contemplating unemployment back in the London winter.

Once a week there were rehearsals for the understudies. I was understudying several roles, and even though we watched the performances each night or heard it from the tannoy (loudspeakers) in our dressing room, we went through our paces. Usually they were conducted earnestly, but occasionally an actor would send up a part by putting his own interpretation on it. Frustrated by the inactivity of understudying and the deadly routine and the already created role, the understudy would find something different to do with the role. The more serious actors had all kinds of tricks up their sleeves and would endeavour to reduce the younger actors to giggles.

Gillian and I were expected to keep in control when actors like Robin Bailey, Jimmy Ottoway and Dinsdale Landon were being wickedly funny.

One scene when I was serving dinner, dishing out potatoes to the dinner guests at a large table, I was to ask how many each would like. They were to reply under their breath as there was other dialogue from the play going on around the table. When I got to Jimmy he said, "Thirteen please," with a straight face. Everyone seated at the table heard his reply, and could hardly contain themselves during the scene.

Fortunately we seldom needed a prompter, even though some of the cast were elderly and had memory problems. The most famous quip comes from, I believe, John Gielgud when he needed a prompt, and when having heard it, he said loudly, "I know the line, but who says it?"

Arriving in Melbourne in the rain we were greeted by the local press, and they began making up stories of how eccentric Miss Hepburn was proving to be. She rode everywhere by bicycle, she spent hours collecting shells on the beach, she wanted to go bird-watching to find the lyre bird.

Helpmann later on spoke of how, after days of hunting, they found several on their last day. Her pursuits were not eccentric, and Helpmann went on to create his well-known ballet for the Australian Ballet called *The Lyre Bird*.

The audiences loved Hepburn and Helpmann together, and the season continued to sell out in Adelaide and Perth. I watched Kate every night from the wings and studied her technique. Helpmann would often stand beside me and do warm-up exercises, ballet movements holding on to a bar or piece of furniture to limber up. He was always there, watching the actors, encouraging them, and his wit used to double us up with laughter at many of the parties that were held in his honour.

The weeks flew by, and when we were ending the tour in Perth, we had a farewell party for Kate, who was flying back to Los Angeles after the last night, Robert going to London. The rest of the company were booked to go by ship back to England, so we had three weeks of ship-board life to adjust to the arrival back in mid-December.

Most of the actors were looking forward to the experience, but several of them, once on board, were unhappy. They did not relish the idea of dressing for dinner every night, or having to follow the dress code on board. One remarked that it was too superficial, and that if he didn't do it at home he shouldn't have to on board ship.

There were no contracts signed for further work with the company as another company had already started work at the Old Vic before our return, so we were all faced with unemployment as soon as we arrived. After our six-month run it was a hard thing to take. With no nightly performances we had become a small family, so it was difficult when we all went our separate ways.

After we got back to London I decided to live in Covent Garden, and during this time I met Stephen Marshall of the Gallery First Nighter's Club.

The Gallery First Nighter's Club, which was dissolved in the mid-nineties, was a club whose members were devotees of the theatre. Up to the 1950s folding stools lined up in rows of four to six were placed outside the theatres for the people waiting to buy tickets for the Gallery. Buskers used to entertain them until the theatre box offices opened. The rows of folding stools quickly filled up.

Before the newspaper critics wrote their reviews, the audience in the Gallery were the deciding factor in the popularity of a new play. They showed how they did or didn't enjoy the play by wild applause or by cat-calls.

Every month the First Nighter's Club held meetings and invited one of the stars from a newly opened play, including celebs such as Noel Coward. They also held special dinners for them that were true "theatrical feasts", and it was very sad to hear that the Club has now been forced to disband because there are no "first nights" in the West End, since each play has previews beforehand. Stephen Marshall, the president of the club, held an emotional farewell meeting at the Concert Artists' Association several years ago.

In this book I endeavour to capture the magic of that area and of its writers and actors who dined in these restaurants during the golden era of theatre in London.

Oscar Wilde said…

I can stand brute force, but brute reason is quite unbearable. There is something unfair about its use. It is hitting below the intellect.

To love oneself is the beginning of a lifelong romance.

Like dear St. Francis of Assisi I am wedded to Poverty; but in my case the marriage is not a success.

I suppose publishers are untrustworthy. They certainly always look it.

The truth is rarely pure, and never simple.

Duty is what one expects from others, it is not what one does oneself.

PERSONAL COMMENTS

Date   Restaurant   Menu   Event

Date	Restaurant	Menu	Event